WRITING WITH

the

Psalms

A JOURNEY IN
NEW THOUGHT

LYNN MURPHY MARK

WRITING WITH THE PSALMS: *A Journey in New Thought*
Copyright © 2017, Lynn Murphy Mark

ISBN (Print Edition): 978-1-54391-760-4
ISBN (eBook Edition): 978-1-54391-761-1

TABLE OF CONTENTS

This book is dedicated to my wife, Jan, who believed

in the possibility before I even dreamed of it.

INTRODUCTION

In 2010 I attended a guided spiritual retreat at a Benedictine monastery outside of Santa Fe, New Mexico. I knew very little about monastic life and the rituals that make a day complete for the monks. While there, I discovered that the Benedictines recite the psalms as integral parts of their liturgy. They do so seven times a day and complete the cycle of 150 of the ancient prayers over the course of seven days, only to start them over again the next week.

Near the end of our retreat we were asked to create and commit to a daily practice that would support the spiritual work we accomplished at the monastery. While walking through the high desert landscape on my way to the chapel on our last day, it occurred to me that I could read one psalm a day and then journal on whatever it called forth from me.

I knew there were different interpretations of the psalms. Rather than search out a particular version, I just wanted to get started with what I had. At the time, the only source that I had at home was my New International Version Study Bible. This Bible and its' Psalter became my companion for the next 150 days. It is the source I have chosen to accompany me on this new journey.

Over the course of five years I journaled faithfully almost every morning. And, I found eight more editions of these prayers written thousands of years ago, prayers that today still express our human longings, fears, joys and sorrows. Not all the editions were from Bibles. Because the psalms are reflective of the human condition, they lend themselves to interpretation, so five of the editions that I studied were written by present-day men and women.

Each adaptation gave me a different perspective on how to interpret the psalms in today's world. I spent nearly every morning in the hours before dawn reading a psalm and writing in my journals. These were kitchen table experiences that turned into a spiritual odyssey. I have eight bound journals, written by hand, complete with lines drawn through phrases and words crowded on the pages.

There were many times when the words flew onto the page, and just as many occasions when I sat with the psalm and waited for a coherent thought to come through me. Some mornings the psalm would eerily fit a circumstance I had just encountered. Other times one would touch a deep place in me that hadn't seen the light of day for years.

I noticed, early on, that these prayers reflect current events. Their application to today is what makes them timeless. Their themes of God's love in times of catastrophic events make them a source of comfort. But the psalms are also prayers of judgment, especially of people perceived to be wicked or evil. The striking part of these Psalms is how much they reflect contemporary human behaviors. It would appear that as a species we have not evolved much where arrogance and bad conduct are concerned!

Several years ago I joined Unity of Naples church in Naples, Florida. Since then I have become a committed student of Unity teachings and principles. With a growing understanding of new thought and metaphysical concepts, the idea of interpreting the Psalms through a Unity "lens" began to take shape. Knowing that Unity thinking stresses the oneness of all, I believe that the Psalter speaks to the common bonds we have with each other and with people who lived thousands of years ago.

As I worked with each psalm, I used Unity literature as my resource. Charles Fillmore, the co-founder of Unity, wrote many books on metaphysics. *The Revealing Word*[1] and the *Metaphysical Bible Dictionary*[2] are two of the books that I used as guides to the metaphysical meanings of the language of the psalms.

The writers of the Psalms faced the same issues of war, oppression, hunger, homelessness, widespread destruction, and political conflicts with which we are bombarded in our daily news broadcasts. They wrote, or sang, to God, asking for answers to difficult questions. Sometimes they were bold enough to demand a solution from God, fully expecting that it would be forthcoming. Often, they were disappointed by God's response, or lack thereof. Who among us has not at times wondered if God was listening at all? And when that happens, where does one turn? The Psalmists' primary answer is, "To God, do not turn away from God."

In Unity, I think we would say, "Look within, to Divine Mind, to Spirit." Unity also teaches the importance of prayer and meditation. The Psalms are prayers and they can also invite us to meditate on their meaning to us personally. They are a rich source of ideas and images. They call us to take a deeper look at our relationships with God, with other people, and with the meaningful events of our lives.

---

1   Charles Fillmore. *The Revealing Word* (Unity Village: Unity Books, 2nd ed., 2006)

2   Charles Fillmore. *Metaphysical Bible Dictionary* (Unity Village: Unity Books, 26th printing, 2011)

Because the psalms became so familiar as I read and re-read them, I have annotated them with personal observations from my journals. My intent is to show just how relevant these prayers are to an ordinary contemporary life. My interpretations are by no means a scholar's exercise. They are simply reflections from a traveler on a commonplace road.

Chapter One

It is a tribute to the Psalms' ability to capture the human condition that so many people have translated, re-written, re-visioned, and unfolded these prayer/songs. Thousands of years after being revealed to a faithful people, they can be meaningful to a person of any denomination or faith.

I have over a thousand pages of journal entries about all 150 of these prayers. The pages capture my comments, thoughts, and feelings about each prayer as the meaning unveiled itself to me every morning. As I wrote this book I reviewed my journal entries and edited them into a personal commentary on each psalm. Because I journaled with so many different editions I was able to see the richness and diversity of the material.

For this book, I chose to work from the New International Version Study Bible[3] (NIV) Book of Psalms. The NIV is my edition of choice whenever I am looking for a biblical reference. I realize that people generally have

---

a "favorite" version, be it the King James, or the New Revised Standard Edition, the New Living Translation, or the Jewish Psalter, just to name a few. Each of these versions reads a little differently from the others, but the essential meaning of a Psalm does not change.

Knowing that reading the Bible is a matter of personal choice, I encourage the reader to take up his or her Bible and compare the language of the psalms with the versions in this book. The way that I chose to write this book was to write my revision of each psalm using Unity/New Thought language, followed by my commentary. I was careful to research biblical terms in the two reference books by Charles Fillmore mentioned in the introduction. With the application of metaphysical language and principles, the re-visioned psalms reveal a gentler interpretation.

For the writers of the psalms, God was an entity "out there" somewhere. God was to be approached with humility, fear, and obedience. Many of the psalms are poignant appeals for God's intervention, because their authors faced difficult circumstances of war, illness, betrayal, vengeance, spiritual distress, and sin. There are also many psalms that address God's goodness and majesty and rule over all creation. Some psalms are written as descriptions of a life well lived in the service of God. Some ask God for the healing redemption for a faithful servant who may have strayed.

Unity thought teaches that God is within me, and that I do not have to reach out to the heavens to contact God. Unity also teaches me that I have personal responsibility for the way I behave and live. When interpreting the psalms with these two factors in mind, their language becomes more inner-directed, and more of a search for that "still, small voice" within each of us.

Most of the psalms have introductory titles called "Superscriptions". They fall into several categories. For example, a series of psalms are attributed to Asaph, thought to be the leader of music in the temple in King David's time. Thus, the superscription reads, "A Psalm of Asaph." Other notations indicate that a psalm is to be used in a particular way during worship. An example of this is the superscription for Psalm 4: "For the director of music. With stringed instruments: A psalm of David." Still others note the occasion for the composition of the psalm, as in Psalm 3: "A psalm of David. When he fled from his son, Absalom".

In the NIV Bible, as in several other editions, the superscriptions are not assigned verse numbers because they are not considered a part of the body of the psalm. Although I interpreted each psalm using Unity principles and language, I left the superscriptions as they are found in the NIV Bible edition. I purposely left them in their original form to give the reader a sense of the original purpose of the psalm.

Over the centuries, as more psalms were written, they were divided into five books which, taken together, make up the Book of Psalms. Biblical scholars give different reasons for these divisions. One scholar, Robert Alter, says this: "The division into five books was clearly in emulation of the Five Books of Moses. Perhaps this division was merely a formal device to help confer canonical status on Psalms, following the precedent of the recently canonized Torah."[4]

Another scholar, Carroll Stuhlmueller, C. P., writes: "For many reasons – practical reasons in order to remember (in an oral culture where most things were passed down by word of mouth and memory) and to preserve (lest some psalms get lost in the shuffle), and topical reasons in order to

---

4   Robert Alter. *The Book of Psalms* (New York: W. W. Norton & Company, Inc. 2007) xix

3

cluster together similar groups of psalms – a new book was attached to an earlier book. Gradually, the one book of Psalms grew into five books."[5]

---

5   Carroll Stuhlmueller. *The Spirituality of the Psalms* (Collegeville: The Liturgical Press, 2002) 5

Chapter Two

BOOK I

Psalms 1- 41

PSALM 1

1 Blessed is the one whose steps are guided by Spirit, whose path seeks to avoid error, whose thoughts are of love and wisdom, 2 who finds joy in divine law, and who enters into prayer day and night. 3 That person is like the tree of life, sending its roots to find God's living water, producing thoughts of a good life and bearing the fruits of spiritual awareness. 4 Not so those who choose to dwell with error thoughts, whose way is unclear. 5 They may not find the path to spiritual understanding, nor will their passage be free from iniquity. 6 For God opens the righteous to harmony and eternal life, but those who support wrongdoing will struggle to find truth.

Psalm 1 reminds me that we are all born with endless possibilities woven into our fabric, and that we all have access to the essential nature of God's truth. This truth keeps me focused on my search for "the next right thing" that lies before me to do. Truth is a signpost for living as cleanly as possible. To stay on the path that this psalm refers to requires me to recognize grace, to be mindful of its presence, and to be grateful for it. That is what is asked of me, to be present in as many moments as possible, to live with integrity and kindness, to use the wisdom that Divine Mind makes available to those who seek it. This is Spirit's inexorable thrust toward growth and new life and the fading of old ways that are not productive.

God invites me to be among the company of those who live with justice and wisdom as their guides. I think about the hymn, "Amazing Grace." The hymn was written by a man who finally found the spiritual clarity that he needed so that he could put injustice and cruelty and self-serving greed behind him. He was a man who was lost, and whose words remind me that, with God, it is possible to be found.

PSALM 2

1 Why do they gather with malice in their thoughts? 2 When the powerful band together to oppose the rule of Divine Mind, they say, 3 "Let us use our strength to release the forces of darkness." 4 God within opposes their anger and their fear, 5 and does not react in kind, rather, 6 seeks to guide them towards the divine plan. 7 God spoke to me in the silence and I heard, "Know that I created you and that we are one. 8 Ask me and I will manifest abundance to you. 9 You will overcome thoughts of conflict and release ideas of loss." 10 Therefore will Spirit guide you in the ways of wisdom. 11 Be of service and study Divine Law. 12 Let love be your guide lest fear weaken your faith. Blessed are those who work with God to invoke good.

Psalm 2 reveals the many ways in which power can be used for both evil and for good. In today's world, just as in the world of the Psalmist, conflict and power struggles are ubiquitous. It is hard to go through a day without being exposed to stories of violence and oppression. It is all too easy for me to become paralyzed by the enormity of issues and causes to be considered.

At these times I must pray in the silence in order to clarify my own responsibilities and accountabilities. When I let myself get caught up in the uproar, when I am contributing to dysfunction of any kind, I must settle myself and listen for God's direction. I cannot quiet the chaos in the world but I can think thoughts of harmony and do my best to behave peacefully in my daily life. As the song about peace on earth says, "...and let it begin with me."

What does God ask of me? It is eloquently expressed in Micah 6:8: "And what does the Lord require of you? To act justly, to love mercy and to walk humbly with your God." (NIV)

PSALM 3

A psalm of David. When he fled from his son Absalom.

1 God, today I find myself beset with worries! My mind cannot safely hold them all. 2 Some say I must look to a distant God for relief. 3 But you, God, are my protector, and I know that we are one. 4 I call on you and you answer me from a place within my heart. 5 You comfort me, and I can sleep feeling the peace of your protection. 6 I will not live as a fearful person because I know that precious Spirit comes to me, and your presence and power surround me. 7 Come quickly to my consciousness,

Spirit! Strengthen me against thoughts of dread and distress.
8 You send blessed relief to all who seek you.

Psalm 3 is a statement of faith. It is attributed to King David at a time when his son, Absalom, was plotting against him and he was surrounded by enemies. As I think about experiencing trouble in my own life, I can identify times when I was given just what I needed to get through a difficult situation. Some things I prayed for, some simply arrived, unbidden yet essential. Some I worked for. Some I had given up on, and when least expected, the blessing arrived.

I have learned that following God's wisdom helps me to clear the obstacles that I place in my own way. Trusting in Spirit helps me to carefully unravel the knots that I create and then I can engage more fully in my own life. In times of trouble, I can find the courage to put one foot in front of the other and keep on moving through. It serves me well to remember that I am "powered by God" from the time that I stand up in the early morning darkness to the time that my head hits the pillow at night. Then there is great comfort in knowing that God is with me as I sleep.

PSALM 4

For the director of music. With stringed instruments.
A psalm of David.

1 I call to you, God, from the place of my suffering. I ask for relief from this sorrow; I look to you for mercy. My prayer is my communion with you. 2 Why, when I do not seek you, am I confused? Then I am tempted to look for the easiest path and I am lured to false claims. 3 Yet I know in my heart that

I am your child; that when I enter the silence you are there. 4 I learn to quiet my thoughts; when I pray I open my heart to the stillness. 5 I know that I must set aside thoughts that do not serve me and that I must trust in your peace. 6 Many people wonder, "Who will make us prosper?". Remind us, God, that your abundance is everywhere present. 7 I am joyful when I acknowledge the prosperity that surrounds me. 8 I am peaceful at the end of my day, knowing that you, God, are my sanctuary.

A little later, in Psalm 46:10, we will find these words of comfort: "Be still and know that I am God." (NIV) Psalm 4 is a plea for release from suffering and worry. In Unity we know that to "enter the silence" is to open to God's restorative grace and to the opportunity to balance the light and the dark in our lives. I would be best served by being still and letting my mind rest from its ceaseless worries.

The thrust of this psalm is the encouragement to trust in God regardless of the outcome. The phrase, "Let go and let God" comes to mind. I know that I much prefer to be in a place of trust rather than in the bog of panic and worry. The times when doubt obscures my faith are times when I stumble. When that happens, I know that I am the one who has turned away from the love that surrounds me. Love is God's unconditional gift to all.

PSALM 5

For the director of music. For pipes. A psalm of David.

1 I enter into the silence, God, because I am troubled. 2 Today I seek the affirmation of your truth that comes with prayer. 3

In the morning, God, I speak to you; in the morning I come to you with faith that I will receive an answer. 4 Precious Spirit, I will not bow to iniquity; with you I find unerring truth. 5 The contemptuous will not enter the silence; those who do wrong do not search for your holy ways; 6 those who deny your truth will not find you. Those who honor violence and deceit are living with error as their guide. 7 But it is through the eyes of love that I can learn forgiveness and enter into communion with you. 8 Let me seek the guidance that Spirit provides as I face any difficulty in my day. 9 I am not bound to live with untruths; I do not need to walk the way of animosity. Nor do I take on an attitude of bitterness. 10 For you, God, wish only good for us even when we stray from your holy ground. 11 When I am in your presence, God, my heart is glad, and my throat is filled with song. I trust that your protection spreads over me and I find myself in a place of joy. 12 Surely, God, I will find the place of perfect harmony when I surround myself with your love.

Psalm 5 is a declaration of faith, a prayer from a devoted servant for whom prayer is an integral part of daily life. This psalm gives me a sense of yearning, of needing to reach out to the One who will always answer in one form or another. The author of Psalm 5 goes to God every day, with a faith-filled heart.

I know that there are times when, without being conscious of it, I enter into God's presence during my ordinary day. My challenge is to look for those moments faithfully, to be aware that I am entering a sacred space. Sometimes the moments are brief, but precious. Sometimes they are revealed in retrospect, before their outcome is known. In quiet reflection about them, they inevitably shore up any part of my faith that might be lagging.

Faith allows us the freedom to wrestle with doubts and turn to God for insight when it is needed. Faith helps us trust that resolution and justice are woven into the fabric of creation in ways that we may never fully understand. There is the passage from Hebrews 11:1 that says, "Now faith is being sure of what we hope for and certain of what we do not see." (NIV)

PSALM 6

For the director of music. With stringed instruments. According to sheminith.[6] *A psalm of David.*

1 God, I know that when I neglect to follow Divine Law, I create discord in my thoughts. 2 Today I am in need of mercy, for I feel weak and my body aches to the depth of my very bones. 3 My soul longs for your healing presence. 4 I must remember, God, to trust in you and to believe that your healing power is at work within me. 5 Those who have been transformed will speak your name joyfully, knowing that there is life beyond the grave. 6 But there are days when I bow to thoughts of illness, and nights when I weep tears of regret and loss. 7 I give in to my fear and I make room for doubt. 8 Then, Spirit comes to me and I choose to set these thoughts aside, and seek the wisdom of Divine Mind. 9 In God will I find mercy, for I am God's

---

6   Sheminith is defined as "The organism of man attuned to the Infinite; the individual living, acting, being, in harmony with Spirit – complete in Him...Man's body is a musical instrument, meant to give forth the harmony of Divine Mind; therefore it must be kept in tune with the Infinite." *Metaphysical Bible Dictionary*, 601.

child; through prayer I will be made whole. 10 Thoughts of disease and imperfection will fall away and I will be restored.

Psalm 6 is one of the Christian church's seven penitential psalms.[7] It speaks of the direct correlation between King David's suffering and his deep longing for God's mercy.

This psalm came to life for me many times when I was a Hospice nurse. It was heartbreaking to accompany someone to their transition, when the person's deep belief was that their illness was retribution for having lived a flawed life. As a Hospice team, we searched for ways to help people cross through this spiritual minefield. For so many people, though, the concepts of penitence and punishment were woven deep into the fabric of their lives. Sadly, even people who had spent their lives performing good deeds fell prey to these debilitating thoughts.

Several years ago I became ill with what could have been a fatal pneumonia. I spent three weeks in an Intensive Care Unit, mostly not in control of what was being done to treat me. I remember one day during which I was not sure that I would survive, or that, if I did survive, I would ever be able to live an independent life. So, the sense of helplessness of the writer of Psalm 6 is not unfamiliar to me.

Chaplains came and prayed with me, friends and family far and near prayed for me, and I felt that God was present within and around me. I decided that the thing that I could do was to give myself over to the care of those who appeared in my room with a job to do. I believed that I was being carried along by love and prayers and the talents of my caregivers. I

---

7   The penitential psalms are numbers 6, 32, 38, 51, 102, 130, and 143.

know, beyond a shadow of a doubt, had I given in to fear and uncertainty I would not have survived.

PSALM 7

A shiggaion[8] of David, which he sang to the LORD concerning Cush, a Benjamite.

1 Precious Spirit, I find you when I am in the midst of controversy, 2 when I am feeling vulnerable and alone. 3 I search my mind and soul for what I may have done 4 to create this turmoil. 5 I consider the consequences of my actions and find that I have had a part in this trouble. 6 Be with me as I change any thoughts that lead me to shame and blame. 7 Help me to live in the world with candor, always honoring you, Precious Spirit. 8 When I bind my thinking to judgment and do not do so with integrity I think false thoughts. 9 I know that I may choose peace, that my thoughts of harmony will produce goodness. 10 You, Spirit, are with me at all times. 11 You keep me on the path of discernment that leads to blessings. 12 If I stray towards error I know that I can find you in the silence; you will guide my thoughts in right directions. 13 You, Spirit, are as close as my next breath. 14 I know that evil must be overcome by thoughts of good and acts of kindness. 15 Should I fall into the ways of error thinking, I can release the ideas that bring chaos and 16 cause dissent to fall upon me. 17 I will live instead with gratitude for all the gifts that communion with Spirit brings to me and I will speak of them with gladness.

---

8   Shiggaion. "A song, ode, or poem that David sang unto Jehovah, concerning the words of Cush a Benjamite…It is of a wild, irregular nature." *Metaphysical Bible Dictionary*, 604.

Psalm 7 has always been a thought-provoking prayer for me. It is about the necessity for self-reflection if I truly want to live with honesty as a basic principle. To do so means looking at my thoughts and actions on a daily basis and seeking guidance from God and Spirit. If I am prepared to listen for this guidance, and respond to the counsel as it comes to me I am more likely to set aside my worn out, stubborn ways, and consider new behaviors.

I could treat each day as if I were standing on the cusp of something new, something pregnant with opportunity. There are lessons to be learned, sometimes not of my own accord, but always with a message and an opportunity to reflect. When I have stopped to consider the bigger picture with a searing kind of truthfulness, I am more likely to see the next right thing that I can do.

The way I see it, the burden of proof is mine, not God's. I may ask for help, or clarity, or insight; I may pray to God to grant me wisdom and courage as I face down my untruths; I may scrutinize my conscience and ask God for forgiveness; but the search for my own integrity is a path I must travel consistently and with a higher purpose in mind. While walking this path I must remember there is not a guarantee of an effortless passage. With God's wisdom, though, I will be guided through a difficult traverse.

PSALM 8

For the director of music. According to gittith.[9] *A psalm of David.*

1 God, Precious Spirit, we listen for your voice wherever we may be, knowing that we are always in the midst of your glorious, infinite Creation. 2 Little children, in their innocence, respond with love when they sense your presence around them. They do not turn away from Creation until they are taught to do so. 3 When I search for Divine Mind, when I enter Consciousness, I see harmony endlessly reflected in the universe. 4 I know that I am a child in your garden, made to flourish in love and compassion. 5 You have given us divine energy to use for good purposes on this earth. 6 We are meant to be stewards of your Creation guided by the movement of Spirit. 7 We are to care for all beings: the animals, 8 the birds flying above, all the creatures in the seas. 9 Precious Spirit, you are within and among all that we see, all that we hear, all that we feel.

For me, Psalm 8 will always be the Creation prayer. It tells me in no uncertain terms that we are all a part of God's Elegant Design. I start with Divine Mind, the substance of the universe. I behold the Divine Idea in the tiniest seed. And, all around me is Divine Expression, whether I see it in the

---

9   Gittith: A stringed, musical instrument. "Soul refinement through seeming trial. The deep peace and harmony into which the soul enters after a seeming conflict has been experienced because of a flow of new life into consciousness, and the consequent quickening and resurrecting of all the forces of the organism into newness of life." *Metaphysical Bible Dictionary*, 238.

riotous green of a Florida landscape, or experience it among the multicolored rocks of a New Mexico high desert.

I have a crystal clear childhood memory from a night during which I couldn't sleep. I went out on to the balcony outside of my room. It was late and I was the only one awake. I was living in Mexico City then, at an altitude of over 8,000 feet. The air was pure and clean and the sky was lit up with stars. I had just read something about the universe being endless, and as I looked up at that night sky, I tried to wrap my child's brain around the idea of "never ending." I simply couldn't grasp the concept of infinity.

Years later, as a student in college, I spent Spring break at the Grand Canyon, while on a science field trip. When I first stood on the South rim and realized how many years it has taken the Colorado River to carve through the sandstone and basalt rock, I had a similar experience of being unable to comprehend the vastness of this canyon and the power of water. I still consider the Grand Canyon to be a mecca of sort, and have been fortunate enough to have climbed in and out several times and to ride the Colorado River and its breathtaking rapids. I always feel the presence of Spirit among the layers of rock that change hues as I hike down into the depths.

Now, in my sixties, I read Psalm 8 with great care. I worry that we have mutated our responsibility toward Creation from stewardship to the dark side of dominion. *The Revealing_Word* says this about dominion: "As a perfect child of God, man is born to complete dominion over all creation. Dominion is an inner consciousness obtained only through mind discipline."[10] There is nothing in those words about carelessness and greed when it comes to living in synchronicity with all life forms.

The last verses of Psalm 8 bring to my awareness the many ways in which we have violated our covenant and mistaken "dominion" to mean "pillage." Often, we exercise our power over the earth and her creatures in ways that are destructive, rather than constructive. Despite all our wonderful manifestations of human thought, we have not always taken the best care of our Earth, our very own little blue planet, spinning in an endless cosmos.

PSALM 9

For the director of music. To the tune of "The Death of the Son." A psalm of David.

1 God, today and every day, I will show my gratitude for your transforming gifts. 2 I will be filled with joy and celebrate with singing in your presence, 3 Controversy and trouble fade away when I am with you. 4 For you have shown me both your truth and the power within me to seek out harmony. 5 Because of you I choose to step away from iniquity and sin. 6 I see the evidence of your works all around me; fear and sorrow fade away. 7 Through your steady presence you guide me to choose truth over falsehood. 8 You are my one and only guide; through you I learn the power of your wisdom. 9 You are my refuge and my strength. 10 All who know of you will be united in your truth, for you are present within us all. 11 My prayers are the songs that I sing to you, and my words speak of you with love. 12 You teach me to reach out to those who are

---

10   Fillmore, Charles, *The Revealing Word*, 57.

suffering. 13 I have no need of anxiety, for you are with me at all times, 14 and I am able to follow your wisdom. 15 Those who knowingly choose error thinking will not find freedom for they will be entangled by their own actions. 16 Spirit, you breathe mercy and justice into me so that I may do your work with love. 17 It is not for me to judge the wicked, but to pray for them. 18 Because you are always with me there is in me a force for healing that can overcome affliction. 19 God, you are a source of endless supply even when my faith falters. 20 Let me not live in mortal consciousness alone, God, for I never want to separate myself from you.

Psalm 9 is introduced as a song about death sung to a melancholy tune. Yet the body of this psalm does not follow along those lines. Instead, there is a recurring emphasis on God's constant pursuit of justice, and God's deep caring for the most vulnerable. God is a protector of the least among us, the poor, the oppressed, or anyone in need of divine intervention.

The psalmist writes of gratitude for God's grace. Although the word "grace" is not found anywhere in the psalm there are plenty of phrases that lead the reader to the transforming power of behaviors rooted in kindness and mercy. In *The Revealing Word*, Charles Fillmore writes about grace, "...if we have ever done a kind act it has been preserved in the careful records of memory and will come forth when we most need it."[11]

---

11   Fillmore, Charles, *The Revealing Word*, 88.

PSALM 10

1 Precious Spirit, I confess that there are times when I am troubled by the world, and when I search for answers, I sometimes don't find clarity. 2 There are those in this world who behave as though there are no consequences to error thinking. 3 In their arrogance, they give in to meanness and selfishness. 4 They think only of themselves and do not wish communion with you. They believe that they have no need of you; their thoughts are not aligned with Divine Mind. 5 Seemingly, they prosper while denying you, and they put aside ideas of union with you. 6 They tell themselves that their strength lies in denial of your truth. They believe they cannot experience ruin. 7 Their words take the shape of lies and they love discord. 8 Their motives are destructive and evil is their watchword. 9 They look for ways to cause harm. Their victims are the innocent ones. 10 They believe in overcoming those who do not agree with them. 11 They want only to live in error consciousness and to never have to answer for their actions. 12 Precious Spirit, help me to remember that the strongest power is the one that works for good. 13 May I remember that wickedness is the path away from you. 14 May I practice compassion and reach out to those who suffer. 15 May I search for your way through adversity, and may I ever speak only your truth. 16 For the way to you is always before me, you wait patiently for me. 17 You, Precious Spirit, are open to those who earnestly search for you; your healing energy is there for all to find. 18 Through faith in your redeeming love, by denying fear, may I affirm your presence and your power.

Psalm 10 is thought to be the continuation and the ending of Psalm 9. Both of these prayers address the dark side of being human and being subject to error thinking, with all of its negative consequences. I find Psalm 10 difficult reading. Going through the litany of mean human behaviors I can't help but search within to find the times when I chose to practice selfishness, or greed, or disregard for what others needed.

For me, Psalm 10 is a reminder of the gift of free will, the inherent right to decide how to live my life day in and day out. With that gift comes the ability to manifest ideas that come from Divine Mind. There is also the responsibility of making choices that affirm good and deny evil. Here is the essence of Psalm 10: it raises questions about the motivations and the end results of behaviors that are arrogant, boastful, selfish, and destructive.

In trying to make sense of this I often find myself on the judge's bench, making decisions about the "what" of bad behavior, instead of considering the "why." When I meditate on this, I try to understand that it is not for me to judge another when in reality I see qualities in them that mirror my own flaws. When I wonder how evil can go unpunished, I remember that I am not privy to the full picture of actions and their consequences. I only see what is laid before me and I have learned that most times the whole story is not available to me. In any case, I can only monitor my own understanding, knowing that I can always enter the silence and be open to other possibilities.

At times, in my search to live out of my own constricted ideas I know that I have hurt others. I have not always been receptive to the lessons inherent in the outcome of my actions. That would require me to make changes that I am not always willing to carry out. Only when I have been disposed to inventory my own conduct have I been able to fully accept the responsibilities that come with an honest heart. This is not always an easy practice for me, but if I want to live a clean life I must be energized by spiritual consciousness.

PSALM 11

For the director of music. Of David.

1 God, in you I find my sanctuary. I am uplifted spiritually when I seek your Divine plan. 2 But sometimes I find shadows around me. Sometimes my confidence wanes. 3 Then I affirm that your Divine Substance cannot be destroyed. How can I not acknowledge its richness? 4 I go to the temple where Spirit surrounds me, and I know that I am whole. 5 God supports the ones who work for right relations in their lives. They do not forget the transcending power of love. 6 God's divine, living, spiritual fire burns through error leaving only illumined thoughts. 7 For God is love, the purest essence of being. When I am open to this love I experience the abiding presence of God and Spirit within me.

Once in my much younger days I was on a solitary hike in the Missouri woods near a beautiful little state park called "Johnson's Shut-ins." I sat down under a tree to rest and get my bearings. I felt the solid ground beneath me and the rough bark of a tree at my back. Suddenly I was jolted by a powerful burst of energy that passed through me down into the earth and I felt an overwhelming sense of connection with Creation. Psalm 11 reminds me that Divine Substance is all around me and that God's spark lies within me.

When I feel the quiet whisper of doubt, I consider the many ways that I am connected to my Creator. I feel the vastness of God's presence, from the farthest reaches of space to the cells of my very marrow, from the cycles of the moon and sun to the dawning of my next day, from the implosion of a star to the time when I will breathe my last in this incarnation.

Psalm 11 tells me to go to the places where I feel Spirit's presence. I am led to trust that God's holy fire burns through the shadows and turns my doubts into ashes. I think back to a time when I thought that seeing was the only way of believing, and I am grateful to have moved beyond that limitation. Now I know that sight is just one of many ways of sensing God's endless love. I can remain open to the pulses of divine energy and recognize the potential for meaningful change and the joy of new thoughts

PSALM 12

For the director of music. According to sheminith.[12] *A psalm of David.*

1 Help me, God, do not let me be in line with a faithless generation; there are so many who think dishonest thoughts. 2 There are those for whom your truth means nothing; in their hearts they hold false claims. 3 They do not enter the silence with you for they speak from self will. 4 Those who say, "My words are my fortress; I have nothing to prove and no one to answer to.", also ask, "Who is greater than me?" 5 Yet Spirit is in the midst of them, bringing words of wisdom to those who might listen. 6 God's words are pure, like silver and gold that have been refined endlessly. 7 You, Precious Spirit, are a place

---

12 Sheminith – a musical term designating the lowest note sung by male voices.

of safety where I can dwell in kindness and not be led to temp-
tation. 8 I am made aware of the pitfalls of human law so that
I may strive to purify my thoughts.

Isaiah was a prophet not afraid to speak the truth about what he witnessed from God's people. In Isaiah 1:16 God speaks: "Wash and make yourselves clean. Take your evil deeds out of my sight; stop doing wrong, learn to do right! Seek justice encourage the oppressed. Defend the cause of the fatherless, plead the case of the widow." (NIV) Isaiah could utter those words today and they would still represent what God asks of us.

Human truth is relative. What I believe to be true is a construct seen through my personal lens on reality. I must be willing to look through new eyes, especially when faced with a truth that I do not want to consider. I must live a life of reflection and discernment, entering the silence, and using prayer and meditation to seek clarity. Otherwise I make room for the falsehoods that sometimes serve as my blinders.

The psalmist tells of human behaviors that are contrary to God's laws of care for creation and for one another. Each of us, however, has the opportunity to be a part of this great endeavor. It is never too late to start. God has no timeline, only the eternal now. There is no beginning or end to God's substance. It is here for us to manifest in ways that support one another and the planet that we live on. When we live into God's Truth, we are at our best, and opportunities to do the next right thing abound.

PSALM 13

For the director of music. A psalm of David.

1 God, I long for your healing touch. When will I sense your presence again? Why do I feel abandoned by you? 2 How long can I live with such pain in my heart when I am unable to reach for you? How long must I struggle with error thinking? 3 Spirit, come to my awareness, bring your light to me lest I become blind to your grace, 4 and those who do not understand my love for you will believe that I have fallen away. They will take pleasure in my misery. 5 But I know that your light brings understanding to my consciousness; your power of redemption brings me joy. 6 I will sing my thanks to you, Spirit, for you are the enduring essence of good.

What a cold and lonely place I am in when it seems to me that God is out of reach. I forget so quickly that God lives within and is as close as my next breath. What I have learned is that I am the one who turns away, not God. When I haven't got the energy to reach out it can seem easier to stay in my miserable state rather than to look for the change that would serve me best. I forget that blessings and trials are the stepping stones of life. I forget that more often than not trials end up as blessings when I am open to Spirit's truth.

It is up to me to remember that when I am vulnerable is not the time for me to insert fear and anxiety between God and me. When I do that, it blocks the channels that allow God's care to flow through me. I close myself off from peaceful requests for healing and, instead, I jump on my personal hamster wheel and start running in place! Only when panic subsides, when I remember to take a deep breath, when I finally feel centered can I open my heart and mind to God's grace, healing, and love.

PSALM 14

For the director of music. Of David.

1 The foolish ones do not acknowledge God. Their goodness is hidden behind evil behaviors; they do not seek redemption. 2 God cannot move through them because of their denials, and they do not honor divine principles. 3 They turn their faces from the light of God's love; there is not one among them who seeks harmony. 4 Why do they stifle their conscience? They reject any sustenance that comes from God; they never seek God's guidance. 5 But dread will come to them for they cannot find a place of comfort. 6 Although they work against those in need, they see that God gives sanctuary to those who suffer. 7 If only restitution would come for them so that they would find the seed of truth! For God's absolution is available to all who seek it.

Many of the psalms are attributed to King David. Whether he actually wrote them all is not known. It is possible many of them were written by poets who knew his stories and depicted them as prayers or songs. In any case, David's life was not an easy one. He fought wars, withstood treachery, and caused his own kinds of troubles. And, he sometimes carelessly disregarded his covenant with God.

David often wrote about his enemies, couching them as godless and cruel. That he himself could mirror these traits comes through in some of the psalms. That he could sit in judgment of others is equally clear, his vision limited to sight through his own wounded lens. In that regard, I have all of this in common with him. I can be quick to make judgments about others. When I do this, I deny the God spark that lives in every one of us. I have no way of knowing what troubles others have, but I need to remind myself that everyone has them.

In Psalm 14, God is portrayed as a distant overseer intent on observing humans behaving badly, asserting their ability to dominate and oppress others. This psalm is a reflection about the misuse of power. These are the kinds of situations that used to lead me to ask how God could allow such cruel and senseless mayhem. There is an answer in *The Revealing Word*, under the topic of "Free Will": "Man's inherent freedom to act as he determines. There can be no perfect expression without perfect freedom of will. If man determines to act in accord with divine law, he builds harmony, health, happiness, and eternal life, which is heaven."[13]

The reverse is also true. Of all God's earthly creatures, humans are capable of negativity. This state of mind allows for a reinterpretation of rules of decent behavior, changing them to suit selfish endeavors and to satisfy greed. Throughout the Psalms we find instances of behaviors that are fractious, disobedient, headstrong, destructive, and disrespectful. The psalmists often ask how God can be so tolerant and remain engaged with us. I believe the answer lies in God's relentless love of Creation, of which we are a small part.

---

13   Fillmore, Charles, *The Revealing Word*, 62.

PSALM 15

A psalm of David.

1 God, is it you who created the idea of our bodies? Did you endow us with the powers of thought? 2 Through the careful use of these gifts we are able to walk in integrity, honor right behavior, strive to speak with heartfelt truth. 3 In your divine plan, we do not speak ill of another, we honor our neighbors, and think only positive thoughts. 4 We do not seek the company of sinners, we honor those who love Spirit, we keep our commitment even when it hurts, and we do not waver in our promises. 5 Through the influence of Precious Spirit we give of our abundance to those who need it; we do not willfully wrong another. If we live in these ways we shall have a strong foundation.

The psalmist asks two question of God, but already knows the answers and eloquently lays them out for us. These are essential questions for people of faith who wish to live fully into God's truth. There are "quiet saints" among us who go about their service with confidence, seeking to do their best for the corner of creation that God has given them to look after. They are the ones whose moral compass is aligned with God's consistent message of love.

I think of Psalm 15 as a sort of job description for living a clean life. The writers of the psalms had Leviticus to use as a guide for righteous living. It is a book of rules so specific that it leaves very little to wonder about. How to dress, how to slaughter an animal, what to eat and when, how to handle a wayward spouse. It is all there, and more.

I think that we each carry a rule book in our heads, one that was given us early on by the people who raised us. These principles by which we are taught to live, by which we shape our lives, do not always fit in the wider context of society. Then we find ourselves with a dilemma. Laws are written to assure that the values of a community are made clear to anyone living or visiting within its boundaries. Like the intent of Leviticus, these regulations are there to control our unruly tendencies, to mitigate our independent streaks, or to create some sort of order in which unlike people can co-exist.

For me, Psalm 15 describes a set of values that can fit anywhere. Look for the next right thing to do. Try to speak out of truth and integrity. Don't gossip, or give out information that isn't mine to give. Honor my neighbors. Avoid wickedness. Keep my promises. Give when it's needed, without expectation of return. Do what I can to help the vulnerable. Be aware and be mindful.

PSALM 16

A miktam[14] *of David.*

When I falter, God, you are my shelter. 2 When I enter the silence with you I know that your presence is everything that I need. 3 I see your devoted servants living from your truth, seeking you always. 4 Those who choose to follow false beliefs cannot live in your consciousness. I will live so that error thinking is behind me, striving only to understand your ways. 5 God, when I enter your realm I can conceive of eternal life.

---

14   Michtam: "The entrance into consciousness of wise, inspiring, harmonious, uplifting thoughts of substance and Truth; and the inscribing of these Truth ideals in the memory." *Metaphysical Bible Dictionary*, 449.

6 Your abundance comes to me in the form of divine ideas; when I study them I am safe and secure. 7 I sing your name with joy; day and night I absorb your love. 8 My vision does not stray from you, God, and I am strengthened in your sight. 9 Happiness prevails when I think positive thoughts; and my body is renewed. 10 I know that you are with me through any transition, and that we will never be apart. 11 God, when I am in communion with you I feel your energy; in your company I am content, because you are my dwelling place.

The first time I read Psalm 16 with real intention a thought came to me: in my life I have been quick to succumb to false beliefs. From verse three to verse four I crossed over from a vision of the saintly servants to the statement about following false beliefs. I thought about all of the temptations to which I have yielded. In my journals, I call them my "little-g gods": possessions, my mental attitudes, my behaviors and anything else that I choose to honor as sacred, while knowing very well that it is not. When I give in to these things I can easily be derailed, and lose my way.

When I am in the midst of the little-g pursuits I give my power away to them. I let myself be swayed into the thoughts of "not enough" and I search even harder for immediate relief. The trap for me is to be lured away from God's promise of abundance and into a mind-set of lack. Despite all the evidence to the contrary, I give in. Sometimes I have managed to set the enticements behind me, sometimes I have learned a lesson from them. Some I have vowed to conquer, and then there are the ones that still plague me. I am grateful for Unity's teachings about denials and affirmations for often they are the best way to mitigate the illusion of insufficiency.

PSALM 17

A prayer of David.

1 I bring my thoughts to you, God, offering the truth as I know it to be. I am in communion with you when I affirm your presence. 2 You bring me comfort, and you set me on a right path. 3 Because you see through eyes of love, you know the best of me. 4 With your guidance I avoid temptation and struggle. 5 When I walk along with you, my feet do not stray. 6 I can turn to you at any time and feel your presence. I know that we are one. 7 When I find comfort in you it is because of your undying love for me. 8 May I stay within your blessed presence, knowing that it is my sacred refuge 9 from thoughts of lack and adversity, thoughts that drain my strength. 10 Let me not follow those who are thoughtless and who speak with disdain in their mouths. 11 When I allow thoughts of error to come into my awareness, I can lose my way. 12 I need the courage that comes when I understand matters of the spirit, then I cannot falter. 13 God help me to move away from those whose tongues are sharp swords. 14 Show me the dark side of wickedness so that I may only seek your light; may I not be led into thoughts of material riches at the expense of spiritual blessing. I do not want to walk in the ways of those who are heartless and wicked. 15 I want only to live in the realm of your divine ideas, for there is the source of all goodness.

There is an old hymn with these words: "Oh there's no hiding place from the kingdom's throne." That concept comes to mind when I read Psalm 17, where the emphasis is on truthful communication with God. When I am in the silence, searching my heart with God's help, I must prepare myself for the lessons to unfold. If I have the privilege of communing with God, then I must have the courage to do it with thoughts of truth. May I also remember that it is not God who needs the cleansing power of an accurate accounting.

When I seek God's presence through prayer I have found that it is best to keep it simple, leaving off attempts to adorn, enhance, or embellish. There is a principle know as Occam's Razor: the idea that, in trying to understand something, getting unnecessary information out of the way is the fastest way to the truth or to the best explanation. When I follow this principle, I keep my prayers simple and give them a clear purpose. That is the best way for me to understand what it is I am praying for.

PSALM 18

For the director of music. Of David the servant of the LORD. He sang to the LORD the words of this song when the LORD delivered him from the hand of all his enemies and from the hand of Saul. He said:

1 I love God with all my heart. 2 God is my foundation, my strength, my savior; whenever I need God I simply go within. 3 I have prayed to God and have always praised God's powers. 4 Once, I feared that death was near, that my ending was in sight. 5 Illness brought me down and dimmed my awareness of life. 6 Friends came to pray with me; they helped me regain my confidence in the power of prayer. I called out to God. 7 God's relentless energy filled me with thoughts of healing. 8 My fear was consumed by God's holy purifying fire. 9 I dreamed that God visited me and told me that love would abide with me. 10 My downcast soul felt the soaring relief of affirmation of God's protective presence. 11 Assurance fell on me like gentle rain. 12 My sight was illumined and my hope increased. 13 My ears heard God's words as if for the first time. 14 I felt a powerful jolt of God's grace run through me. 15 The depth of my fear was revealed to me. 16 God reached for me and soothed my anxiety. 17 I began to deny the power of illness. 18 I affirmed that my body was strong and that my health would be restored. 19 My breath grew strong and my heart opened up to the healing presence of Spirit. 20 Because I was able to affirm that my life force was strengthened, my healing progressed. 21 I have kept my deep faith in God's power of protection. 22 Divine ideas are mine to study, I need not turn away from them. 23 I will not give in to error thoughts. 24 I have been rewarded with an attitude of reverence, and my thoughts are clean. 25 Faith begets faith; hope begets hope. 26 The pure in heart will see God, but the wicked will not. 27 You reward humility, but arrogance gets nothing from you. 28 When I meditate, I am enlightened; darkness disappears. 29 With positive affirmations I can overcome any distress; I can climb to new heights. 30 God's perfection is a shining beacon to those who would increase the strength of their spirit. 31 God, and Christ ideal, and Spirit are one within me. 32 From God comes fortitude of body, mind, and soul. 33 With God I can walk through my life secure, I can raise my thoughts to a new awareness. 34 I am given what I need to make my life productive, praising God in the process. 35 With God and with Spirit my life is enriched. The possibilities multiply as I meditate on them. 36 The path before me is straight and my way is clear. 37 I set my error thoughts aside, and replace them with thoughts of abundance. 38 I do not associate myself *with negativity; I look for the good around me. 39 I feel God's energy flowing through me; I am able to accomplish my goals. 40 When I am in the middle of conflict, I look for ways of resolution. 41 If someone is in need of help I offer what I have. 42 I do not turn my back nor do I add to their difficulties. 43 I look to God when I am troubled and I have found answers in unexpected places. 44 New things do not frighten me, but I am careful with them. 45 I do not wish to live from a place of fear. 46 I am glad about the steadfastness of God. 47 With God I am able to accomplish more things, 48 things that will be of benefit to my surroundings. 49 For all of this I give my thanks to God. 50 In return, I am richly blessed by God's love forever.*

One thing that comes to me when I read Psalm 18 is this: if I am not looking for God in the details of my life, I am looking in all the wrong places! This is what my relationship with God is all about. I trust in God's presence in me, in my surroundings, in all of creation. God above and beneath; God to the right and to the left; God behind and ahead; God in the four directions; God in water, air, earth and fire; God in the nebulae and in the atoms. I ask God to open me to all of the places where God is, starting with my own existence.

Despite all of God's gifts there are times when I paint myself as a little holier than thou. I have depicted myself as the heroine, taken the credit for deeds well done, narrowed the limelight so that only I fit in it. The thing is, in so doing I have tarnished the truth, and there is no virtue in that. If I have learned anything from reading these Psalms it is the knowledge that God's Truth trumps mine every time. When I follow God's requirements to seek justice, to love mercy and to walk humbly with God (Micah 6:8), there is no need to portray myself as anything other than a simple soul moving through God's creation.

PSALM 19

For the director of music. A psalm of David.

1 From the realm of pure ideas to their manifestation on earth may God's glory be praised. 2 With the daylight comes greater understanding; even at night does knowledge pour forth. 3 Not with words nor with speech does enlightenment express itself. 4 The laws of creation make manifest God's harmony. Even the sun has its place. 5 It follows a steadfast course day after day. 6 Its beginning in the morning and its light throughout the day give warmth to the earth. 7 Divine law is there for the spiritual seeker to find and in so doing to grow in understanding. 8 God's principles are pure sources of joy. God's commandments promote the holyness in us. 9 When Divine Law is approached with reverence and awe, the pure in heart will know God. 10 By seeking to know Divine Mind we are given gifts of the spirit; God's wisdom is always revealed. 11 Those who seek to know Spirit will experience great delight. 12 May I deny the power of error thinking and seek forgive-ness when it is called for. 13 May I direct my will away from temptations that do not serve me; only then will I be free from false claims. 14 Precious Spirit, may the thoughts in my mind and the contemplations in my heart be expressed in service of your good.

The psalmist tells us that God's wisdom does not always require words to communicate with us. As I behold a star-filled night sky, words cannot give proper measure to the sight. Only my soul can escape this planet's gravity and seek to travel among those points of light so very far away. Any words I hear come from my own being, trying to find a voice to describe what I witness, awed by the fact that I am observing only a miniscule piece of the universe(s). Although we now have a much greater understanding of the science of creation, the humbling part is that we still only understand a small fraction of God's cosmos.

The vastness of the firmament calls forth faith in things unseen and not completely understood. Psalm 19 tells us that God's laws always lead to harmony. Believing that God is the creator of All That Is, why would I not want to seek and follow God's guidance? God's precepts are restorative, reliable, just, and pure. Why would I not choose to absorb these gracious gifts and seek to live within their circumference?

Unlike the psalmist, we have access to the findings of astrophysicists. We hear the terms "black holes," "dark matter," "holons," and "Higgs Bosons". We know now that our own sun is a humble, old-ish star, a modest presence among the galaxies. And yet without its light our versions of life would not exist. The psalmist likely would have been astounded to know what a miniscule corner of creation we occupy. What might they have thought about a Creator who took millions of years to set the exact combination of atoms in motion that resulted in a single cell life form? The same Creator who let millions more years elapse before crawlers became four footed who then became two footed and learned to stand mostly upright?

We are advised to approach Divine Law with awe. I am encouraged to sharpen my senses and my awareness, to have an eagerness to learn.

When I enter the silence with reverence I am open to epiphanies. Once I get direction and know how to proceed I am apt to get a little jolt of joy at a newfound sense of purpose.

PSALM 20

For the director of music. A psalm of David.

1 I look to God when I am apprehensive and unsure of my next steps; I seek the protection of Spirit. 2 I go into the place where God and I commune and I find peace. 3 With God's help I clear my uncertain thoughts; I create a place for new ideas and I renounce my fears. 4 I deny all thoughts of lack, and I affirm God's abundant blessings. 5 I find my strength in joy and I celebrate God's goodness. 6 I know that God's grace pours over me when my soul is open to it. Answers come to me in the form of affirmations. 7 Some trust in the allure of the material world, but I seek Divine Mind's immovable truth. 8 Those who trust only in the mind of man will falter, but I am firm in my belief in God. 9 When I am governed by Spirit I cannot fail! My call is heard and honored.

Every Sunday at Unity of Naples we end service with James Dillet Freeman's "The Prayer for Protection." It is a powerful affirmation of God's omnipresence. These are its words:

"The Light of God surrounds us. The Love of God enfolds us. The Power of God protects us. The Presence of God watches over us. Wherever we are, God IS...And all is well!"

I have this prayer on my little home altar where I see it every day. It brings me great comfort to know that God is as close as my next breath. Through these words I place my trust in God, and wait with gratitude for the grace that comes from my Creator. I learn to keep my senses wide open because grace comes in so many forms and I do not want to be closed off from any of it. This does require me to look beyond the borders of my life and trust that what comes my way is intended for good use.

Psalm 20 was very likely to have been written as a prayer to be said before entering into conflict. It serves just as well as a prayer to be said at the beginning of my day. It reminds me that I am not alone as my day unfolds, and that the presence of Spirit is not to be taken for granted. This does not mean that I sit back and wait for God to "handle" my difficulties. Instead, I can remember that I am in partnership with the God of my understanding. I am always invited to seek the thoughts that come when I open up to Spirit's direction.

It takes a certain amount of spiritual discipline to live this way. When I neglect to examine my impulses before I act on them; when I let impatience take over instead of using prayer and reflection; when I ignore my intuition in favor of a quick fix; then I am forgetting God's Light, Love, Power, and Presence.

PSALM 21

For the director of music. A psalm of David.

1 Precious Spirit, I give thanks for your presence and power in my life. 2 You teach me to trust that goodness is mine for the asking. 3 I celebrate the gifts that come with your presence. 4 With you comes a way of life that is filled with endless spiritual energy. 5 When I live according to your truth, I am richly blessed; my consciousness is open to you. 6 In your presence I am filled with joy and contentment. 7 I am strong when I am guided to seek Divine Mind principles. 8 I can think positive thoughts and forego false beliefs. 9 When I am troubled, I can affirm that I am in tune with spiritual harmony. I can be open to purifying thoughts and seek to attract only good. 10 Any thoughts of lack can be set aside. 11 I can change my thinking about adversity and I do not need to consider evil. 12 I can turn away from error thinking. 13 I lift up my consciousness to you, Precious Spirit and my words will tell of your blessings.

There is often a careful order to the ideas expressed in a psalm. For example, right at the center of Psalm 21 is verse 7 considered to be the most important statement in the midst of all the others. Verse 7 says that I am at my strongest when I give myself over to the teachings of Divine Mind. With God as creator of All That Is I can believe that there are laws of physics, chemistry, and biology in place that keep the cosmos running smoothly. I have only to listen with receptive ears, and see with perceptive eyes, and be willing to find new information to use for the betterment of my corner of creation.

My belief is that God is always present within and without. This thought helps me to practice patience and discernment as I search for the next right thing to do. As my day unfolds I sometimes have to guard against finding blame for any adversities. That kind of thinking leads me on paths that are treacherous and prone to self-pity; paths whose destinations are not places where I want to linger. There is no comfort to be found there. I must remind myself of the ever-present power of choice, meaning that

I always have the opportunity to make decisions that are in synchronicity with divine law. I can look for ways to be helpful instead of choosing to stand in the way of a positive resolution.

PSALM 22

For the director of music. To the tune of "The Doe of the Morning." A psalm of David.

1 In my most troubled times I fear that God has turned away. I call out from a place of anguish and desperation. 2 By day I enter the silence and find no response; at night I cannot rest from my weeping. 3 In my struggle to find God I search my heart, the place where I have always found divine guidance. 4 In the past my confidence in God and Spirit has always upheld me. 5 I have shared my deepest hopes with God and my trust has never been broken. 6 But now I am at my lowest ebb. There is no one to turn to. 7 When I look outside of myself I find no consolation. 8 "Trust in God", is what others tell me. 9 I know that God is my Creator, 10 that I have known of God since before my birth. 11 I pray that I may feel the presence of Spirit around me, for I am faltering. 12 I look for strength in places where I have found help. 13 I pray for courage, that I might overcome what is plaguing me. 14 But all I feel is weakness in my spirit and weariness in my bones. My heart is heavy. 15 No words of comfort come to me, nor can I speak my own prayers for health. 16 Wherever I look I cannot find hope. 17 My frailties are evident to all who know me; they cannot help me. 18 My possessions are of no comfort to me. I would give them away if I could. 19 But you, Precious Spirit, do not keep a distance from me. I need your sustaining grace to hold me up.

20 I need relief from the thoughts that frighten me. 21 I cannot live among them. 22 I speak your name, Precious Spirit, I seek you among my familiars. 23 I know that I have been filled with awe when I am in your company. 24 I feel like an alien as I search for you; I have always found your comfort before. 25 I am trying to find words that will bring peace to my mind. I want to praise your healing presence. 26 I want my poverty of spirit to be fed so that I can be of strong heart again. 27 I wish for the overwhelming peace that comes when I find you in the silence; 28 for your divine plan includes us all. 29 No one will be left without hope. I pray for that for myself so that I can look toward the future. 30 Today I cannot look beyond this hour, 31 but I will keep walking in faith, expecting relief.

Psalm 22 is long and painful to read. Its writer looks for relief and cannot find it, despite a belief in the power of God and Spirit. I can feel this person's sense of being isolated from the comfort of God's presence. Whether that abandonment is self-imposed is not clear. The writer moves back and forth from the hopefulness of entering into prayer with God and Spirit, to the desperation of feeling forsaken. The psalmist knows about the soothing nature of God's love, but somehow feels estranged from it, surrounded only by the darkness. I can understand the fear and pain because I have been in such darkness myself.

My times of anguish happen when depression seeps into the crevices of who I am, and I start to turn into who I am not. It is subtle in its onset. I know when it is coming because my wider world starts to fade from view and loses its allure. I begin to fold into myself as the unwanted cloak wraps itself tighter around me, obscuring my view and narrowing my thoughts. Past and future hold little meaning as I cannot extend myself backwards or forwards, so I exist in a few square feet of uneasy psychic space. Like a tongue probing a sore tooth, my mind carefully tests my surroundings looking for my misplaced sense of purpose.

How easy is it for me to lose confidence in God's grace when I am this sick and afflicted? This is my struggle when depression comes on me. I am so wrapped up in my discomfort that I give up on looking for relief from God and from Spirit. Only afterwards, when my life has been restored, can I see the many ways in which God's help arrived. Through the actions of others on my behalf, God's grace is apparent to me. I know that their prayers surrounded me when I felt alone; people came to me when I could not invite them; my spouse stayed by my side when I could give nothing back. I understand then that God was at my side every moment, keeping me as safe as I would allow and holding on to my hope when I could not find it.

PSALM 23

A psalm of David.

1 God is the source of all that I need. I am complete. 2 I may enter the silence where I find Divine Mind, and where the peace of Spirit prevails. 3 God breathes new life into my soul. I am given what I need to learn of the next right thing to do in God's name. 4 When I find myself in darkness, you surround me with grace and you stay by my side. I have nothing to fear. Your wisdom and your love are my greatest comforters. 5 You show me my capacity even when I doubt myself. Your words soothe me and give me hope. 6 You fill me with goodness and mercy wherever I go, and I shall live in your enduring creation forever.

I believe that somewhere, at this very moment, people are using this prayer to comfort, to give solace, to start the long journey to closure after someone's loss. Psalm 23 is recited at bedsides, at gravesides, in churches and cathedrals and basilicas and temples. I have been in congregations where we take a collective breath and slowly sink into a moment of surcease, a temporary suspension of raw grief, as these gentle words wash over us.

The message in Psalm 23 applies in so many circumstances. Beyond its usual appearance at times of great sorrow, it carries a lesson about the times on our journeys when God's gift of mercy calls us to do right: make a stranger feel welcome; give away what I don't need; sacrifice something for someone else's welfare; stand up for kindness; respect all, myself included; appreciate the gifts that come from God and share them with others.

Then there are times when I need courage to face what is coming. Dark times spare no one. I don't think that it is possible to navigate through life without encountering fear, or gut-wrenching sorrow, or the razor's edge of loss. There will be disappointment, goals unmet, promises broken, unmerited anger, lost friendships, deep family rifts, false assumptions. There will be white-knuckle days and nights. Loneliness and despair may eat away at spiritual peace. This is when I trust in God to lead me to the other side. The words of the 23d psalm give me the assurance of hope.

Walking this path with God sometimes requires the slow yet constant progress of putting one foot in front of the other, and keeping my eyes on the road ahead. The steady rhythm of forward movement, neither a crawl nor a race, helps me to stay centered. I can open my senses to receive God's careful guidance as I move forward through my day.

Psalm 23 is the invitation into prayer and meditation where troubled hearts are soothed and at least a part of the path ahead is made visible

PSALM 24

Of David. A psalm.

1 God, all that we are and all that we have belongs to you. 2 We were created in the waters of life and are carried on their divine substance. 3 We are able to ascend to an exalted state of mind. We can live in spiritual wholeness. 4 As I develop spiritually I gain understanding of the Christ Mind that dwells in all. I do not give in to false claims. 5 Because I trust in God, I experience prosperity in all areas of my life. 6 When I seek you, Precious Spirit, I receive inspiration. 7 I remain alert and ready to be guided and directed in the ways of goodness. 8 When I am in God's presence I am free from doubt; my strength of body, mind, and soul increases. 9 I find the place where I can express creative thoughts and ideas. 10 To whom do I turn? I turn to the eternal I AM.

Psalm 24 is a glorious elegy to God's Creation and to our place in it. Because we are given the gift of thought and of words we are capable of expressing beauty in so many ways. The arts, and other works of our hands and minds, strive to reproduce the elegance of God's cosmos. We know, on some level, that we are made of the same stuff as the stars and we are led to assemble this stuff in ways that honor Creation.

A few years ago I sang in a small choir in Santa Fe, New Mexico. It was in the season of Advent and we were preparing music that would mirror the depth and beauty of the Christmas miracle. We sang a song with words by the poet, James Agee. The words spoke to me of a person so taken by the wonders of the night sky and the call of the universe that all he could do was weep:

"Sure On This Shining Night" by James Agee

Sure on this shining night
Of star made shadows round,
Kindness must watch for me
This side the ground.
The late year lies down the north.
All is healed, all is health.
High summer holds the earth.
Hearts all whole.
Sure on this shining night I weep for wonder
wand'ring far
alone
Of shadows on the stars.[15]

How often are we invited to look up at the sky, or at the soaring heights of a mountain?

As we experience the creative power of Divine Mind we have the opportunity to climb to higher ground and see our surroundings with new eyes.

It occurs to me that we might start that climb when we take our first breath of the air that envelopes the planet. Along the way we may be taught lessons about clean hands, and pure hearts, and the power of truth. We may be left to make these discoveries on our own. As children, we watch

---

15   Fitzgerald, Robert, ed. The Collected Poems of James Agee, (New York: Ballantine Books, 1970) 7.

carefully what happens around us, in our living spaces. We absorb the messages, the behaviors, the words people use, words that are responsible for shaping us. The black and white and shades of gray of life are laid upon us at a very early age. Through the grace of Precious Spirit we begin to see other colors, muted or brightly hued; we begin to hear other notes, sharps or flats, dissonant or harmonious; our fingers learn to feel shapes and textures. And off we go to create a life of our own surrounded by God's presence.

PSALM 25

Of David.

1 In you, God, I have the highest confidence. 2 My trust is unshakeable; in your presence there is no shame, only blessing and honor. 3 Because my faith in you is strong, I am able to overcome error. 4 I look to you for guidance so that I may walk in your ways. 5 Your eternal truth is my source of hope for the future. 6 In the beginning there was your love and your mercy. 7 You show them to me and you forgive the indiscretions of my past. 8 The door to your kingdom is always open, an endless source of good. 9 You teach me to approach you with humility, for I alone can accomplish nothing. 10 When I live lovingly and faithfully I am upholding our covenant. 11 I can humbly ask for forgiveness when I have behaved in error. 12 Who am I to approach God with anything but reverence? God is my greatest teacher. 13 Your abundance will endure throughout the generations. 14 With you there is no fear, only awe when I enter into the silence. 15 When I have burdens of my own making, I look to you for help. 16 When I am alone with my troubles, I pray to you. 17 Through the workings of Precious Spirit I find relief from my unhappiness. 18 I can meditate on the right way to ease my mind. 19 I do not need to give in to false claims. 20 I can find peace in the silence as I pray for guidance. 21 You lead me on the path of truth and integrity, and I place my faith in you. 22 May I enter into spiritual consciousness with you so that I may demonstrate your truth.

Psalm 25 is one of my favorites. Reading it, I remember that every day I have a chance to start fresh, to remember my place in God's Creation, and to live into the challenges of my humanity. I am assured the Christ nature within me brings endless possibilities for living with integrity in all aspects of my life. I can acknowledge my mistakes and seek guidance, or forgiveness. When I pray to God I ask for balance in my life, so that light and shadow are in harmony.

I ask to remember that humility is a pathway to God and to my soul's freedom from ways that no longer serve me. Perhaps they never have served me but I was reluctant to let go and to give them over to God. If I am not paying careful attention I can so easily stumble into a snare. It is inevitable that I will trip over my transgressions. However, if I have been aware of past indiscretions, I can use the lessons learned from them and I can commit to God that I will be more careful in my discernment.

Psalm 25 promotes hope in the future, and faith in the present. Hope in its purest form does not guarantee the outcome that I wish for. But it is a great source of strength and wisdom. Faith is that powerful energy that moves life forward and can be the undoing of any obstacle. Hope gives a breadth of vision. Faith brings with it the ability to see beyond turmoil and to believe that the power of good is ever present.

The other theme to be found in Psalm 25 is that of forgiveness. The purest form of forgiveness comes from God, if only we are open to it. I remember reading a book about St. Francis of Assisi, one of the most humble of God's servants. He struggled mightily with shame. He held many a dialogue with God about his shortcomings and his flaws. Despite his faith, however, he did not always emerge from these sessions convinced of his goodness. He suffered because of the power of his own doubt and his inability to forgive himself. Psalm 25 tells me that forgiveness is a merciful balm for the one who practices it and the one who receives it.

PSALM 26

Of David.

1 I come to the silence, God, with the assurance that my faith and trust in you has not wavered. 2 My life is lived with integrity and I open my heart for you to examine. 3 I am aware of the emanation of Divine Mind throughout Creation; and I rely on your steadfast love. 4 I do not seek false beliefs and I live without honoring false claims. 5 When I encounter evil I turn away from its disharmony; I do not live among the unwise. 6 I seek to live using principles of good, and I enter your sanctuary often. 7 I go there to listen to your word and to learn of your good works. 8 When I am in your presence, God, I find that peace and joy abound. 9 I will seek your presence through prayer and meditation, so that I do not lose sight of your wisdom. 10 I stay away from scheming and plotting, for there is nothing to be gained from them. 11 I want to live a life free of reproach; I ask for your mercy when I stray. 12 I live with a strong foundation, and I will praise you in your sanctuary.

This is a psalm from a person with the confidence that comes with living a clean life, comfortable in the knowledge of God's steady presence. There is contentment that comes with practicing denials and affirmations and cultivating a purity of thought and spirit.

I have learned that I can open myself to God's scrutiny without fear of retribution. My faults accompany me into the silence as much as my attributes do. Through prayer and meditation I can turn my faults into teachers, and look for the lessons that accompany them. I can use God's words to reform my will and make the effort to change my behaviors.

The poet relies on the comfort of entering God's sanctuary. In this world there are so many forms of such sacred space. Some are ancient, some are glorious achievements of architecture, and some are simple rooms with little adornment. Some are huge and imposing. Some are rustic structures. I have seen many different kinds in my travels and in my places of residence.

In Northern New Mexico there is a very holy place some distance from Santa Fe. It is called the Sanctuario de Chimayo. It is known as a place where healing occurs, the kind of healing that leads people to set their crutches aside and walk without them. On Good Friday people walk from many miles away, making the annual Easter pilgrimage to Chimayo. I remember very clearly my first visit there. I approached it as a tourist would, examining its plain exterior, the small flagstone courtyard that leads to its door, and the door itself, made of dark and weathered wood.

As I opened the door and entered into the quiet space, I was not prepared for the half gasp, half sob that flew out of me when I crossed the threshold into the dim coolness of the small sanctuary. With tears flowing from my surprised eyes I sat in a very old pew for what might have been a half hour absorbing the simplicity of this place. Other people came in quietly and genuflected in front of the rough-hewn altar. I knew that, for all the lavish cathedrals that I have been in, I have never had God's grace cup my soul like that.

Those are the moments when nothing else matters and there is no interference between my Creator and me. They are moments filled with unimaginable reverence. For me they are usually brief interludes. I am grateful when they happen, but I know that living in the grip of such awe for more than a few ticks of the clock takes a strength that is reserved for saints and mystics.

PSALM 27

Of David.

1 God is always with me – why would I need to be afraid? God is my strength and my protector – who can threaten me? 2 When I am faced with evil of any kind I turn away and pray for release. 3 When I am in the presence of conflict, if I have caused the turmoil, I can ask Spirit to show me the next right thing to do. 4 There is one thing that I ask for from God: that the living words of Divine Mind guide me to health in body, mind, and spirit. 5 When I am troubled, communion with God is my place of safety; in the silence my consciousness is uplifted and I feel confident. 6 Then my thoughts rise above those of the material world and are refined. Old beliefs fall away. 7 When I pray, I go to a sacred space, I let go of negative thoughts. 8 In your presence, Spirit, I seek only good. 9 I think only about God's abundance that is always available and will be manifest through good works. 10 When the realm of material things fails me, I find comfort in meditation. 11 My mind seeks purity and I turn my thoughts to God's divine plan. 12 I have no need of false beliefs that make me doubt my own abilities. 13 I believe that I can find God wherever I look by affirming God's presence in this world. 14 By listening to Spirit's voice I find myself closer to God.

To believe God is within me is to appreciate the importance of optimism, that peaceful feeling that, at my core, all is well. No matter the circumstances, God is present. I am free to look for the good that surrounds me. Should I find obstacles, God is closer than ever. I use the tools of denials and affirmations: Denials are a powerful way to refrain from and release negative thoughts and self-talk. Affirmations reshape my thoughts and experiences in positive, supportive ways. By using these methods I can effect changes that help me to enter directly into enlightened consciousness.

Denials and affirmations take me on a journey to a safe place from which all manner of sorrow, remorse, guilt, resentment, and self-pity can be released. I gain insight into old, useless ways and see that I no longer need them. I can hear the persistent call to a healthier way of life in all spheres. I start to see beauty reflected in my surroundings, my relationships, my work life, and in myself.

I believe that it is the search for enlightenment that matters. I take a daily journey through the hours, watching thoughtfully for God's imprint. I look at my role in what is taking place, and when I am in an uncomfortable situation, I discipline myself to look for the wider view and to be open to guidance from Spirit. I remember the importance of contemplation that gives me the ability to avoid jumping to conclusions and to temper my tendency to judge. Only then am I truly open to be led by Spirit.

PSALM 28

Of David.

1 I call out for you, God, and I wait for your answer. As I wait, I set aside thoughts of fear and resistance. 2 I listen for your message while I seek your help. I pray to be restored. 3 I take my place as one of your children, and I imagine your goodness surrounding me. 4 I do not want to harbor thoughts that block any healing. I ask for greater understanding of my faults so that I may release them. 5 When I give in to negativity, I pray for an awakened conscience so that I may manifest your good. 6 I know that with your truth I am able to change my thinking. 7 With you, God, do I find courage. I trust in your love, and in your help. 8 When I think of you, I am confident in your healing power. 9 You are the source of all forgiveness and you will never abandon me.

For me, prayer is an exercise in patience. If I am calm and willing to listen with a discerning ear, any answer that I need will come to me. I do not know what form it will take, or the time frame in which an answer may arrive. Sometimes, though, the quiet that lingers before the answer comes is the time needed for preparation and creation of a receptive space that is free from distractions.

Sometimes prayer brings the unexpected. I hear the words, "Be careful what you ask for!" I know that in the past my prayers have been answered in ways that caught me off guard or brought lessons forth that I could no longer ignore. These may be the answers that hold the most value because they come from a place beyond my sight, from a power far greater than mine, from the wind of Spirit that envelopes all Creation.

Thoughtful prayer is my opportunity to live a better life. It is a chance to ask for clarity, and awareness of those times when I am not my best self. These are the times when I am drawn to a mean behavior, when my thoughts are pronouncing judgment on another, when hurtful words come out of my mouth, when I walk by another person's need without a thought of stopping.

Prayer is also a time to step away from a distracted life. Smart phones, computers, television, iPads, all of them draw me toward the ceaseless noise that contributes to commotion in my soul. In fact, prayer may be the most effective self-help activity of my day!

PSALM 29

A psalm of David.

1 When angels speak they say that all things are possible with God; that unity and strength will prevail with God. 2 To God goes the glory. When we seek to join with God - Divine Mind - we are made whole. 3 Through God's voice, the formless and the formed are manifest. 4 God's decrees are clear and with them come blessings. 5 God's majestic voice speaks only words of purity. 6 Through Divine Mind comes the sublime announcement of Creation. 7 Through that powerful expression the realm of human thought is changed. 8 God's word creates thoughts of abundance and good. 9 The power of God's divine energy runs throughout creation and manifests itself in glory. 10 Streams of God's eternal living water flow through the cosmos. 11 Through God comes our strength; through Spirit comes peace.

The psalmist writes of the power of God's voice and how it moves Creation in ways seen and unseen. As a child, I believed that thunder and lightning and big winds were the voice of God. I still revere the powers of nature that can both destroy and build up. I imagine the noisy cataclysmic events that take place out in the universe. Stars imploding or exploding, black holes sucking in light, planets in the making, all speak to me of Divine Mind's abiding ability to turn substance into stars.

In *The Revealing Word*, Charles Fillmore defines voice: "The power center in the throat controls all the vibratory energies of this organism. It is the open door between the formless and the formed worlds of vibration pertaining to the expression of sound. Every word that goes forth receives its specific character from the power faculty. Therefore, the voice is the most direct avenue of expression of consciousness."[16]

If we, as humans, can give such substance to our thoughts and abilities, what awe is required in considering the dynamism of God's voice? This is the God that prevails by the still waters, the God that exists in the midst of tsunamis and earthquakes.

We call huge natural events, "acts of God." Often wherever this happens there is loss of life and property. Such catastrophes may leave us with the difficult question, WHY? With today's sophisticated scientific technology

---

16   Fillmore, Charles, *The Revealing Word*, 205.

we can explain the HOW? Tectonic plates shift and Mount Everest is moved. Wind forces gather together and swirl into a tornado. The ocean floor separates and a terrifying wall of water is formed. We know the HOW of these events. The WHY often goes unanswered.

Poets and theologians and philosophers are given the challenge of explaining the WHY. For me, I can only enter into communion with God and seek some understanding when I listen for that "still, small voice" within. This is the voice that speaks to me in the midst of tragedies and blessings and helps me to make some sense of them. If I do not get an answer right away I know that I can keep looking for understanding through prayer and meditation.

PSALM 30

A psalm. A song. For the dedication of the temple. Of David.

1 I will praise you, God, I will turn my thoughts to your saving grace and think about your help in times of trouble. 2 I turn to you, God, I bring my thoughts in line with your goodness and I am restored in health. 3 When my spirit is at a low ebb I know that I can reach out to you. 4 I tell those around me that my thoughts of you make me whole again. 5 When I study your ways I learn to temper my anger; my sorrow may last the night, but joy arrives with the dawn. 6 When I meditate on the divine plan I feel secure. 7 When I am in communion with you I am on a firm foundation; when I struggle to connect with you I am disconcerted. 8 Then I call out to you, and I ask: 9 "Where can I turn if not to you? How shall I proclaim my faith in you? 10 Hear my words with merciful ears, God, be my help." 11 Through prayer my troubles turn into opportunities; my fear turns to courage. 12 I will give thanks through song and words of praise. You are with me forever.

I deeply appreciate Psalm 30's optimism about the power of connecting with God. I know where to find the true source of joy and it is in the ability to reach for God's wisdom. Why I would choose to turn away from the affirming energy of my Creator is a question to which I know the answer. It is a result of laziness of spirit, a trap in which I sometimes find myself.

When I am in such a state I'd like to be able to say that God is unavailable. This is when I most need to be anchored to God, while I ride out the storm that surrounds me. What happens instead is that I can become so self-absorbed that my faith is on temporary hold. It becomes as listless as the rest of me. There is no logic to my thoughts and I create a mental climate of doubt that is of benefit to no one.

To come out of the darkness of confusion into the light of clear direction holds an immeasurable joy. It is the relief of arriving at a decision that feels right and to make a plan that promotes integrity. Sometimes the choices come to me suddenly; sometimes I agonize over the options, until I remember that it is a privilege to have options. I have been known to plunge into a half thought out, half-baked "plan" of action. And, I have learned the hard way that sometimes those are the ones with the best lessons.

I don't always know when God's grace has pulled me out of the way of oncoming traffic. Faith tells me that this has probably happened more times than I will ever be aware of. In return, however, I understand that the responsibility for my own wellbeing, my own sense of joy, is something that I must nurture through prayer, through the study of Unity principles, and through frequent experiences in the silence. I have opportunities to correct what I have done, accept the consequences and learn something of value.

PSALM 31

For the director of music. A psalm of David.

1 When I turn to you, God, I am safe; you will lead me to a place of tranquility where I may experience your goodness. 2 When I am troubled, I call to you for help and I ask to be lifted up. 3 Because you are my haven I can trust in your guidance. 4 Give me insight, God so that I may not fall into a trap of my own making 5 I turn my life over to you. 6 I keep my distance from those who proclaim falsehoods, and I put my trust in God. 7 I find comfort in your presence, for you understand my distress. 8 As I meditate I know that you give me all that I need. 9 And yet I ask for release from the discomfort that plagues me, that makes me weak and sorrowful. 10 Help me to release these thoughts of anguish and despair. 11 Sometimes I feel as though people who surround me have rejected me and turned their backs on my grief. 12 I feel broken and unloved. 13 My thoughts lead me to a state of fear for my very life. 14 I wish only to affirm my union with you, my God. 15 I place my life in your hands and I pray for redemption. 16 Manifest in me the evidence of your unfailing love. 17 Send Spirit to me with a cleansing breath of life so that I may strive to correct these thoughts that trouble me so. 18 Let me not give any more power to the negative state in which I find myself. 19 Instead, help me to affirm that in you there is an abundance of love, and that I can change my thoughts to reflect goodness. 20

May I remember that faith in you surrounds me with your protection. 21 May I praise the ways in which I can set aside despair and think only of your manifest love. 22 Although I have felt estranged from you, I have only to deny my fear that you have abandoned me. 23 I affirm that I am always connected to you; that when I doubt, I am the one who leaves you. 24 When I turn my thoughts to you I find my source of courage and strength.

The message found in Psalm 31 is always one of faith in God as a shelter and a refuge in times of trouble. It is clear to me that I must put forth the effort to find relief, no matter how pained or disturbed I am. I know that I can communicate in the silence, and open my heart and my soul to God's grace. I have an inner voice with which I can give word to my distress. In so doing, I can deny the heaviness of shame and ask for lightness of spirit. I can remember that God's enduring presence is always within me and surrounding me.

Unity teachings tell me that it is important for me to access the power of God that lives in me. I don't have to look outward to find God's love. I can call upon inner wisdom, sometimes using past lessons to see my way more clearly. I can rearrange my thoughts to make room for new ideas about living for the next right thing. I don't have to be bound by old thoughts of shame and regret.

Shame is a great secret keeper. Shame is a deep hole in my soul where I store bits and pieces of my story, the parts that I never want to be discovered. Shame is where I hide my transgressions, cleverly concealed, hoping always that I will forget where they are hidden and thus be rid of them. But it isn't that simple. If I dwell too long in my hall of shame, my perspective is skewed and I am not in a position to learn from my wrongs. When I feel cut off from God, when I can't open my soul to God's scrutiny and ask for forgiveness or redemption, I cut myself off from the possibility of renewal.

There are times when any forward motion is impeded by my own sorrow. I get in my own way and spend time dwelling on the negative. This is a waste of precious time that gets in the way of affirming that God and Spirit are right there with me. What comes to me then is something that I have heard and believed for years: This too shall pass. If I am to honor my faith, I must trust in the rhythm of my days and know that some are trickier than others, but that all of them are blessed.

PSALM 32

Of David. A maskil.

1 It is a true blessing when I am able to face my own errors and ask for forgiveness. 2 I bring my sins into the light of scrutiny and I am willing to change where I must. 3 When I live in isolation with my transgressions my heart grows heavy. 4 When I am not honest with myself I cannot reach for God's truth and I grow exhausted. 5 I come to God ready to reveal my dark thoughts; I confess into the silence and wait for God's healing grace. 6 I pray that others may express faith in God and find release from negative thoughts.7 I know that I am protected in your presence; I can let go of wrong thinking and be filled with thoughts of harmony and peace. 8 I trust that you will teach me to find the right path that leads to your wise counsel. 9 I pray that I will let go of stubborn ways that keep me from living my best life. 10 When I think of the presence of evil in the world I am secure in the knowledge that I have no need of wickedness, that my enduring trust in you opens me to your love. 11 I find joy and gladness in you, God, and I will praise you with song and prayer.

Whenever I read Psalm 32 I think about the 12 Steps used in recovery. Those Steps address life spinning out of control as the result of repeated harmful behaviors. The Steps require careful personal scrutiny in the face of continuing spiritual erosion. I believe the essence of this prayer speaks to a relationship with God that allows for a real accounting of my shortcomings.

When I am able to open heart and mind to divine scrutiny I become more honest with myself and better able to think clearly about my next steps. Throughout the psalms I find reasons to believe that God already knows my strengths and my weaknesses. Trying to hide the truth over the long term is an exercise in futility. It is not for God to keep me honest. I have everything that I need to do that through prayer and meditation. And, it is not enough to simply admit my misdeeds. If I look at them and do nothing to correct them then I am mired in error thoughts.

Reading the words of this psalm helps me to appreciate the freedom that they offer. There is a great burden lifted when I acknowledge that my self-will is out of control. Then I can decide to make changes, with the help of God and Spirit. I can honestly look at the areas where error thinking has obscured my judgment.

Sin is a sticky concept, subject to individual perception and interpretation. The Bible is filled with the cause and effect of sinful thoughts, behaviors, and actions. Whole chapters are devoted to rules designed to help us distinguish between transgression and right behavior; elaborate systems are in place that allow us to seek absolution. Forgiveness of sins and the mandate to set things right are examined in the light of the Cross and in the complexity of Karma. Psalm 32 teaches me that trust in God and a willingness to change lead straight to a saving grace.

PSALM 33

1 I sing to God from a heart filled with joy; it is right to praise God with songs. 2 Music comes forth from stringed instruments played for the glory of God. 3 A new song can be found each time God is sought. 4 I know that I will be closer to God when I open my soul to creative endeavors. 5 God is present in the midst of right actions and of justice; God's love can be felt at these times. 6 Divine Mind is the source of all that is and the breath of Spirit moves the spheres in the heavens. 7 God gathers the waters of life and sets us among them so that we may have vitality. 8 Let us all gather with awe at the sight of God's creation; let us approach God with great reverence. 9 For the word of God gives order to all things; God spoke and the universe came into being. 10 God guides our thoughts toward right actions. 11 God brings consciousness to those who have faith, whose belief in Divine Mind is unwavering. 12 God brings our faculties into focus so that we may bring ideas to full expression. 13 God is omnipresence and omnipotence; mankind is God's holy idea. 14 There is no place hidden from God's sight. 15 God breathes life into each heart, and never leaves the soul alone. 16 The world of material things is but a manifestation of God's abundance; there is no power greater than God's. 17 Even the power of human thought, which gives expression to ideas, is no match for God. 18 But God sees the

*hearts of those who revere the expressions of Divine Mind. 19
God's love delivers us from evil and reverberates through eternity. 20 It is good to hope in God, for God is our protector. 21
God's truth is never far from our consciousness; 22 and God's
grace is all around us.*

As the psalmist writes in the opening verses, music is an open doorway
through which to approach God. Music goes straight to areas in the brain
where creativity flourishes, where communion with God can happen on
a deeper level. Some of my most hopeful prayers occur when I am singing with my choir or listening to someone perform and express his or
her talents.

Growing up, there was always music in our house. I believe, in retrospect,
that music took the place of any form of worship in a church. We were not
participants in any organized group of practitioners of faith. I did not learn
about gathering in God's name until much later in my youth. It happened
for me when I joined the chapel choir in college and my whole perspective
toward worship changed. From my place in the choir loft I was immediately drawn to God by the beauty of the notes and the lyrics and the blend
of human voices.

Psalm 33 speaks to me of God's magnificence. The writer tells us that every
encounter with God and Spirit holds great creative power. I know how
much more alive and resonant I am when my intentions are in line with
creation's ceaseless movement. Honoring the potential in me and in creation opens so many possibilities for the expression of my talents, whatever they may be. When I open my heart to God I am given what I need to
further God's work in my corner of the world.

PSALM 34

Of David. When he pretended to be insane before Abimelek,[17] who drove him away, and he left.

1 I will speak highly of God and I will express great thanks for God's goodness. 2 I will seek to join my being with God-Mind and affirm God's healing powers. 3 I will invite others to join me in seeking God's will. 4 I have gone into the silence with God and have been strengthened. 5 Those who search for insight and clarity are rewarded with new ideas. 6 Someone gives up thoughts of lack or poverty and finds abundance in God. 7 Precious Spirit surrounds us with love and we are spared from wickedness. 8 Open your senses to the gift of substance; find all manner of blessings throughout creation. 9 Approach God with reverence and awe and you will lack for nothing. 10 When your spirit wanes enter into communion with God and find courage. 11 Seek always the spirit of truth and you will find comfort there. 12 When you wish to live a good life, 13 refrain from speaking harshly and use words of truth. 14 Do not pursue wickedness, but be gentle with others. 15 God lives within us all and knows when we need counsel; 16 God leads us away from evil. 17 Even the strong in heart will cry out to God; Precious Spirit will answer. 18 In times of difficulty, prayer can reverse the darkness and healing thoughts will take its place. 19 Troubling times can be changed by meditation and thoughts of resolution. 20 Divine Mind is the source of our protection. 21 We will not be brought down by

---

17 Abimelech: "This Abimelech stands for the intellectual thought or tendency that accepts and acknowledges God as the supreme ruler in man's consciousness." *Metaphysical Bible Dictionary,* 15.

wickedness; error thoughts will be replaced with right think-ing. 22 God is our shepherd; we have nothing to fear.

Psalm 34 is filled with phrases about living of life of faith in God and Spirit. The writer urges us to start by praising God, and then issues invitations to join in the pursuit of life lived fully through relationship with God. Living in such a way is to believe absolutely in God's goodness; it is also a daily opportunity to study each manifestation of God's infinite patience and compassion. There is much encouragement to look for the expressions of mercy that come from God and from Precious Spirit. All that is required is that the seeker turn toward God with reverence and awe, and turn thoughts toward the certainty of abundance.

So many of these encounters with God and Spirit are sacred moments. Yet, I know that I live much of my life in ordinary time, paying attention to the details of a daily routine. I am prone to forget about the power of awe. When I remember to be reverent I live as though at any moment I might encounter some precious phenomenon of God's creation. If I live daily with this intention, making it the rule rather than the exception, how much richer would life be? How much more likely would I be to find the quiet joys among the mundane?

How often in my lifetime has God's grace intervened to lift me up? I won't ever realize the entirety of this saving grace because, in addition to being unconditional, it is often invisible and undetectable when it happens. This is exactly why gratitude should absolutely underpin my attitude.

PSALM 35

Of David.

1 Today I need respite from my troubles; come to me quickly Precious Spirit. 2 Those with sharp tongues speak out against me and I am in distress. 3 Lift me up out of harm's way; be with me through this trial. 4 May I seek greater understanding of my circumstances so that I can deny wickedness and have no part of it. 5 May the redeeming breath of Spirit surround me; your truth will set me free. 6 May the consciousness of sin be removed from my awareness. 7 May I not be drawn in to error by thoughts that do not serve me. 8 May I choose only thoughts of my highest good. 9 Then will I rejoice in the beauty of Divine Mind. 10 And I will take comfort from knowing that my consciousness is expanded beyond my present situation. 11 When I am faced with untruths may I turn them away by affirming the goodness of Spirit. 12 I do not need to choose evil when it crosses my path. 13 Instead, I can enter into the silence in search of Divine ideas. My prayers will open me to thoughts of compassion. 14 I have offered help where it seemed to be needed. 15 If my actions are denied in the presence of wickedness, I can always turn away. 16 I cannot make choices for another. 17 But I can find the courage to turn away from negative thoughts. 18 For this gift, God, I am grateful and I will speak using only words of peace. 19 I know there will be times when others speak ill of me. 20 Let me not be drawn in by their false claims and untruths. 21 I do not need to believe in that which I know to be wrong. 22 I need the strength of your presence to guide me. 23 You are around me and in me, God. May I ever be conscious of your support. 24 Lead me in ways that promote peace and harmony. 25 Help me to affirm that this unhappiness around me is not mine. 26 When I am in the company of those who wish me ill, help me to deny their power over me. 27 May I be a faithful witness to the gifts of affirmation and peace. 28 My words will be rooted in wisdom and I will praise you all day long.

The writer of Psalm 35 is someone who is experiencing the sting and pain of betrayal. Circumstances lead the writer to make an impassioned plea for God's intervention in a difficult situation. Having asked God for help, the writer asks if there is anything that can compare to God's deliverance. The forces at work against the psalmist can only be reined in by God, whose energy always favors justice and righteousness. Where else to turn to but to God? Coming from a deeply wounded place, not knowing who to trust, the psalmist writes a long prayer asking for justice and relief.

When I have experienced deception and dishonesty from others, my first reaction is often one of simple bewilderment. A few times in my life people that I have loved and trusted blindsided me in ways that I never would have predicted. Then I struggled with the WHY of it all, wondering how someone could act in such a way. On those occasions when I did not think to turn to God for thoughts of resolution, I found myself in a place of anger and allowed that anger to take root in my being. On anger's heels came sadness that a relationship might be damaged beyond repair. Eventually I found that I could forgive, but somehow not forget. Therefore, the rancor, now muted, still lived in me. What might have occurred had I turned to God and prayed for guidance? I suppose it's never too late to do that. But by now I must ask for forgiveness for myself for hanging on to judgment for so long.

Entering into a quest for resolution by praying and meditating on the possibilities can only lead to a good outcome. More than likely I will find myself in a place where I need to examine my own behaviors that may have contributed to the trouble, uncomfortable, but necessary if I am to find the truth of a situation. For me, this can only come through careful self-examination; through seeking counsel from a trusted person; and ultimately by going to God for an answer.

PSALM 36

For the director of music. Of David the servant of the LORD.

1 I learn about wicked people when I hear their words of hate and injustice; they do not have a reverence for life. 2 Their eyes are blind to their own error. 3 Their ears are deaf to their own iniquity. 3 Their words attract evil to them; they do not walk in the ways of compassion. 4 Their days and nights are filled with thoughts of error; they act in ways that promote wickedness. 5 But your love, God, is overarching and available to all who are faithful to you. 6 Your divine law operates on principles of justice and harmony. You, God, protect all your creation. 7 There is no price on your unending love. You are a haven to those who seek you. 8 Your spiritual nourishment is abundant; you surround us with your living water. 9 Your healing presence invites us into connection with you; with you we find enlightenment. 10 When we look for you, we find our consciousness elevated. 11 Your wisdom guides us away from temptation, and we do not stray far from you. 12 May we deny all evil and affirm acts of goodness.

The first four verses of Psalm 36 speak about people who are seemingly estranged from God's goodness and compassion. From that point of view, power over others becomes a goal, entitlement is a way of life, and greed replaces mercy. This is how oppression takes root, how hatred becomes a driving emotion, and how causing damage to other human beings turns into an acceptable activity. If this weren't so, we would not see so much evidence of it when we turn on our devices to get the daily news.

In my 45 years as a nurse I have taken care of hundreds of people in all kinds of settings. As a nurse, it was incumbent upon me to approach people with an open mind, and a desire to discover what kind of help they needed or wanted. The vast majority were good people, just trying to do their best in the midst of illness or injury. There were some rare occasions, though, when I cared for people whose eyes were flat and did not reflect a recognizable emotion. From experience I know that there is a story behind this phenomenon of empty eyes, and I can only imagine how disturbing the details may be.

Sadly, as a school nurse I saw this three times in the thousands of visits with students who came to me. I remember exactly who these children were because of the heinous nature of their life circumstances. I would get an outline of their short life story and encounter details of sexual abuse, domestic violence, drug and alcohol use, parents in prison, chronic homelessness. And in the worst case, it was all of the above carved into a young psyche. It seemed inevitable that a vicious cycle was in the making.

But the writer of Psalm 36 devotes the majority of the verses to the ways in which God is accessible to anyone who wants to live a clean life. When I have had my fill of sorrowful news I remember that I believe in God. I believe in the laws of creation. I know that goodness exists in people. I believe in free will, and I believe that it is subject to misuse. It can open me to behavior that is flawed and dangerous. But, the opposite is true as far as choices I can make that reflect compassion and a basic caring for others, regardless of their circumstances.

PSALM 37

Of David.

1 Avoid the company of those whose intentions are evil or who revel in error thinking; 2 their influence shall not last long, for their actions will fade with time. 3 Put your trust in God and seek only goodness; live a clean life and your blessings will be manifested. 4 Find joy in communion with God and Spirit and your heart will be happy. 5 Dedicate your life to God and you will enter the kingdom. 6 As the sun rises and shines through the day, so will your contentment show forth. 7 Enter into the silence with God and pray for good; do not envy those whose riches come through wicked deeds. 8 Study your anger and you may find a blessing; ease your thoughts and seek their lessons. 9 Those who persist in error ways will be diminished, but those who follow God will prosper. 10 The wicked will wander in the wilderness and they will be gone from your sight. 11 Those who answer wrong with love will flourish. 12 Those who are filled with wrath behave in the ways of anger; 13 but God's love is always available to them. 14 Some use sharp words to injure others, they do not wish them well. 15 But their words and actions will come back on them. 16 Better to humbly love God than to dwell with negative thoughts; 17 for the error thoughts have consequences that must be faced. 18 Be content with your affirming thoughts and your days will be joyful. 19 In times of trouble your way will be made clear and you will receive what you need. 20 Even the wicked can be purified and their evil can be burned and consumed. 21 Avoid those who take and never give back; but give freely of your gifts. 22 When you do so you will find blessings from God. 23 When you love God your steps are firm on God's path; 24 you will not stumble for God's mercy supports you. 25 I have seen with my own eyes how God's sustenance is given out to all who wish to receive it. 26 Those who receive this bread of life learn to give generously to those in need. 27 Those who turn away from evil will access the kingdom of God. 28 In the kingdom will they find divine law; justice will be their calling. Error thinking will find no place in them; disturbing thoughts will fade away. 29 They will use their attributes for good. 30 Their ability to discern will grow and they will seek justice. 31 The voice of God is within them and they will persevere. 32 Temptation will present itself but they will not be deterred. 33 They will continue to learn from God and God will protect them from harm. 34 They will expect good to come their way and it will be manifested. 35 Though it may seem that the wicked flourish, in time they must face God and explain their iniquity. 36 Their evil ways will be diminished. 37 Learn from those who pursue truth; whose actions strive for peace. 38 They will turn away from sin and seek redemption. 39 They will be free from limitations; God will be their shelter from trouble. 40. God is always to be trusted to hold their highest good whenever God is sought.

The forty verses in Psalm 37 clarify the difference between the wicked and the righteous. They speak of what it takes to seek the highest good: always trust in God, do good works, live blamelessly, repay debts, give generously, seek justice, speak wisely, be a person of peace.

There is much in this prayer about patience, about wading through trouble and turning to God for help. I am encouraged to acknowledge that evil and wickedness do exist but that I need not give in to them. There may be temptations to seek an easier, softer way, which can make me careless in my actions. I am called to live a life of good deeds, and carefully think about the consequences of my actions. When I do so, I am more likely to behave in ways that recognize injustice and I can choose not to participate in it. Sometimes this means that I must wait patiently for the next right thing to reveal itself.

The message that I get from Psalm 37 is that accountability for my own actions is important in my life. It is so easy to look around and find ways to distract myself from the only life that is under my "control." When I have erred, I must learn from this experience and refrain from repeating it. It really is that simple and it is not always easy. Building on my relationship with God requires that I examine my actions and motivations in the context of fairness, justice, and kindness. These aspects of God's grace exist with or without my participation, but I know at my core that I want to live in the flow of that precious energy, and that I want to contribute to it as well.

PSALM 38

A psalm of David. A petition.

1 God, I fear that I have fallen away from you and my mind is filled with dread. 2 In my mind, you too have turned away from me. 3 Because of this my health is in decline; I can find no comfort anywhere because of my transgressions. 4 I remember how long I have lived with thoughts that are untrue. My burden is heavy. 5 My soul is wounded and my very being is repulsive to my eyes. 6 My energy is at its lowest ebb; I can hardly move. 7 I live with constant pain and I find no relief. 8 I have become weak in body, mind, and spirit. 9 God, I pray to you without success; surely my efforts are apparent to you. 10 My heartbeat is erratic, I grow weaker with each day and the light has faded from my countenance. 11 There is no one around me who can help. 12 I sense the presence of death nearby; my thoughts have become negative whispers of illness. 13 My ears do not hear goodness coming to me and my voice is silenced. 14 My senses are dulled. 15 God, I long for your truth; I wait to hear your answer to my pleas. 16 I struggle to change my thoughts so that I may once again hold you closely in my mind. 17 I need your divine guidance to move my thinking toward your goodness. 18 Instead, I am overwhelmed by my sins. 19 I have turned away from those whose company would be a balm for my troubles. 21 God, I pray to be lifted up in consciousness; I long to be close to you again. 22 Help me to remember your affirming words so that my life can be restored.

Sometimes in the course of a life well lived come moments of despair and alienation. When those moments turn into hours, or days, their burden is relentless. The writer of Psalm 38 is suffering. As the words spill across the page, they imply that this person is close to death. Perhaps it is not a physical death, but a spiritual one that is happening. It seems as though the writer believes that somehow he or she has failed God, that perhaps the burden of sin is so heavy that God cannot be reached.

I know how it feels to sink so low that I believe that I have created a wall around me that is impenetrable, even by God. In my arrogance, I believe that I have the power to turn God away!

I remember reading about Mother Teresa's life, about how she came to be considered a contemporary saint on the fast track to official sainthood. For all the good that she did, and for all the lives that she touched and changed, she struggled with doubt and despair. She experienced depression much of the time. Her accomplishments were driven by her convictions, her kindness, and her quest to live by God's truth, but her heart and mind were troubled.

In Myrtle Fillmore's book, *How To Let God Help You*[18], she emphasizes that the search for God's Truth is essential in maintaining any level of health of body, mind, and spirit. She writes, "From the beginning, all of the qualities and capabilities you need in order to make for yourself a perfect destiny have been implanted in you. Through your study, understanding, and practice of Truth principles you are finding how to awaken, develop, and set free into righteous expression all of these inner spiritual resources."

PSALM 39

For the director of music. For Jeduthun.[19] *A psalm of David.*

1 I will measure my words before I speak them; I will avoid expressions that are hurtful. 2 In the presence of error I will

---

18   Myrtle Fillmore. *How To Let God Help You*, 23.

19   Jeduthun: "The spirit of love, joy, and praise vibrating exultantly through the whole consciousness of man, and playing upon every center in his organism, establishing divine harmony." *Metaphysical Bible Dictionary*, 327.

speak only of your Divine Law. Otherwise my spirit suffers. 3 My heart wants to use words of love. If I speak ill of someone, my heart grows heavy within. 4 God, I want to live my days using your abundant life force. 5 I do not dwell on thoughts of when my death will come; I have no way of knowing the length of my years. 6 If I thought of nothing but my ending, I would gather material goods around me and forget that love is my destiny. 7 Instead, God, I will remember the eternal power of life. 8 I will meditate on your divine energy and use it throughout my days. 9 I will enter the silence and seek your wisdom. 10 I will contemplate abundance, and manifest it wherever I go. 11 I will replace thoughts of wealth and material goods with gratitude for the breath of life that is your gift to me. 12When I pray I will release sorrow and guilt and replace them with affirmations of your truth. 13 If I ever doubt you, I have only to meditate on your presence within me. My unsettled thoughts will disappear.

When I read Psalm 39 I have two thoughts: one has to do with silence, and the other is about the end of life that we each must experience.

As for silence, I know that there are times when it is best to confine my words and opinions to the space between my ears. I think about the times when my mental "filter" has failed me, when words best left unsaid come hurtling from my mouth, not to be taken back. And, there have been many times when I should have spoken up, and out of a desire to avoid controversy at all costs, I have refrained. This usually leaves the issue unsettled and unresolved. At times like these I need to ask God for the courage to speak what I believe to be the truth, for the resilience to listen carefully to the response, and for the flexibility to change my assumptions.

In *The Revealing Word*, Charles Fillmore writes, "Death, first and second – The first death is the death of the light and life of Spirit in man's consciousness. The second death is the cessation of vital force and action in the body. It occurs when the mind completely loses control of the body. The functional activities cease, and the physical organism dissolves."[20]

Every Palm Sunday I have a vision of Jesus entering Jerusalem, holding the sure knowledge that the death of his body was imminent. Jesus was not given an old age, or even a middle age, with which to continue his mission: he had to know that each day was a precious opportunity to teach about the kingdom of God. I think back on my Hospice days and remember that there were so many times when people asked to know, "How much longer?" Sometimes the question was asked in an effort to treasure each dwindling moment; sometimes it was asked as a plea for relief and release. Some transitions were predictable, while some defied all odds. And, on some occasions, a person would turn a corner back into a full life.

What I know for sure is that God gives me each day to open my eyes and make a plan for how I intend to use the gift of another day. That is both a sobering thought, and a cause for rejoicing.

PSALM 40

For the director of music. Of David. A psalm.

1 I meditated in the quiet and God's truth came to me. 2 My discomfort was removed and I felt secure. 3 I sang a hymn of praise to God. I came to God with awe and reverence and I trusted in God. 4 I am blessed because I seek to know God,

---

20   Fillmore, Charles, *The Revealing Word*, 50.

and I turn away from false beliefs. 5 I have been a witness to mighty things, things that are done through faith in God. 6 I refine my consciousness and make room for new thoughts. I offer my best life to God. 7 God is the Absolute, I need not fear what is to come. 8 I have learned that God's will for me is all good. 9 I speak freely of God's abundance; I do not hesitate to tell anyone about it. 10 In my heart lives a righteous intention to speak only words of God's truth. 11 I trust in God's unending mercy; I have felt God's love at work in my life. 12 At times, I am troubled by my own iniquity, when I have closed myself to God's presence. 13 Then I remember to pray to God and release such thoughts. I know that God is as close as my next breath. 14 If there be anyone who wishes ill for me, I will pray for them. 15 I will look upon them with kindness and not give any power to their negative thoughts. 16 I will join with others who meditate on things of the spirit. 17 And though I may falter at times, I have only to seek God's guidance, and my steps will lead me on the path to truth.

Psalm 40 is one of praise to God, and gratitude for God's unswerving support. It is also about my responsibility to live out of a sense of abundance and grace. Where just about anything is concerned, grace brings redemption. I do not dispute that God's grace is more than capable of doing the heavy lifting, but this is not to be done without my conscious participation. In fact, it should be one part grace to nine parts of effort from me. I must also be aware of how grace brings just what I need, just when I need it. My part is to recognize God's guidance when it appears, regardless of the whisperings of my stubborn will, and to follow it to the best of my ability.

Unity teachings reinforce the power of affirming God's good intentions for me. What I need to do is to pray for the resolution of negativity into positive thought, and anything is possible. I know this to be true from a recent health experience that I had. For reasons unknown, a tendon in my left foot suddenly ruptured and broke away from the bone to which it was anchored. It happened just six months after bilateral knee replacement surgery, from which I was still recovering.

I went to a foot doctor who told me that I would need surgery to replace the tendon and secure it back where it belonged. At that time, the thought of more surgery and confinement was more than I could handle. I got the information about the consequences of not having surgery, and thanked the nice doctor for his help.

Instead of opting for surgery, after much prayer and consideration, I decided to work with God by consciously designing a recovery program for my foot. It involved a series of exercises, and a lot of time in a pool using a swim fin to strengthen the muscles in my foot. A year later I went back to the foot doctor for a follow-up appointment. After examining my foot he told me this: he did not understand exactly what I had done to heal my foot, but the end result was better than anything he would have achieved with surgery.

With God, all things are possible.

PSALM 41

For the director of music. A psalm of David.

1 Blessings upon those who care about the powerless; God gives them relief when they need it. 2 God sends the redemptive breath of Spirit to the weak – their innermost thoughts are strengthened – and their energy is transformed. 3 Error thinking that causes weakness is reborn as thoughts of soundness. 4 I once asked God for mercy and for healing; my iniquities had overcome my thinking. 5 Thoughts of illness preoccupied me and my faith faded away. 6 Negative images came to me and I began to fear for my life; I told my companions that I was afraid. 7 Those who did not really know me spoke about my weakened state and believed that I was damaged. 8 Their words carried nothing good about me; they believed that death would come for me. 9 I sense that even those closest to me have lost confidence in my ability to heal. 10 Come to me, God. I will open myself to Spirit's cleansing power so that I may be restored in body, mind and soul. 11 I will seek your truth about my life and I will transform illness into health. 12 Because I believe in the power of your works I will change my thoughts into powerful messengers that carry healing to all parts of me. 13 I will praise you, God, for ever and ever. Amen

When I read Psalm 41 I am taken back to my time as a hospice nurse. This prayer describes so much about the commonality we share in the face of illness. From the patients and families that I cared for came a new understanding of the idea of "healing." For them, the definition of healing did not always match the inevitable outcome. What I experienced in those days and nights was to learn that healing does not always come to the body, but may manifest as a spiritual renewal, or a repair of a fractured relationship, or a doorway to communication that is finally opened.

Myrtle Fillmore was a remarkable woman. She found herself in a nearly deadly struggle with tuberculosis, with an apparent decline that could have led to her death. The following passage from her book, *How To Let God Help You*, helps me to understand how she turned her state of disease into one of health.

"No one who has awakened spiritually and is seeing his threefold being in the light of Truth speaks of disease as something of itself. He does not think for a moment that the mind is fixed in old race beliefs or errors, or that his body is unresponsive to Spirit. He ceases to think even of the name the doctor gave to the condition. He casts out and forgets their assumption that this condition could not be changed and done away with utterly, just as you would refuse to hold and to think of some unworthy or untrue thing you might hear spoken as you walked down the street.

Then, he begins to rejoice that he is an offspring of God. He declares that the Life and the Substance of his body are the perfect pattern of that life and body which are the gifts of God. These gifts are in reality inseparably one with God's own Being, the very essence of God-life, God-Substance, and God-Intelligence. It is God's plan to have the creation express His own ideas, qualities, and being Man's work is to become conscious of and to express in his life the true pattern and qualities of God."[21]

---

21 Fillmore, Myrtle, *How to Let God Help You*. 122-123.

Chapter Three

BOOK II
Psalms 42–89

PSALM 42

For the director of music. A maskil of the Sons of Korah.

1 As a forest creature searches for water, so my soul longs for you, God. 2 My soul thirsts for your living water, for your holy streams. Where can I find them? 3 I weep many tears because I yearn for you; people ask me why I search so hard to find you. 4 Even though I go into your holy house there are no shouts of joy there for me. 5 I fear for my soul for it exists in the depths of my despair. My God, I reach for the hope that I have found with you before. 6 My thoughts carry me to places I do not want to frequent and I long for a higher state of being – I want only to open my consciousness to your truth. 7 In my weakness I have strayed from you; I am in a state of unrest. 8 By day I feel more secure, at night I listen carefully for your song of praise – I raise up my prayers to you. 9 You have been my foundation, but I fear that I have forgotten how to find you in the silence. 10 My whole body aches; I can hope, and pray for release from this suffering. 11 Why is my consciousness at such a low ebb? Why am I so uneasy? Although I falter I will keep seeking communion with my God.

The writer of Psalm 42 reminds me that I have had times when I have felt disconnected from God, and disconsolate. I have asked myself if God has somehow disappeared. Thinking back on these occasions I know that they are characterized by a fear of abandonment on my part. This promptly paralyzes my spirit and closes my God eyes. This is when I most need to trust that God does not turn away from me. God lives within and when I emerge from my state of doubt, this assurance is immediately available to me. I remember that my participation in this creation dance was never guaranteed to be without its difficult steps and mysterious rhythms. There will be setbacks, and I will feel discouragement. How I use these inevitable happenings largely determines the outcome. I am in a much stronger position when I work with God, not against God.

Psalm 42 is also a precious prayer in my life. I read it at the Homegoing Celebration of my first hospice patient. I even call this one, "Lillye's Psalm" because every word of it took place during her journey to her transition.

Lillye lived in a rough side of town. She had a severe mental illness complicated by a history of alcohol abuse. When I saw her for the first time in the hospital I was sent to her because she also had a very advanced stage of breast cancer. Her daughters met me outside of her room and advised me not to use "the C word" because Lillye refused to acknowledge that the huge mass in her breast was malignant. Lillye had refused all treatment, and by the time her daughters had gotten her to agree to go to the hospital, there was really nothing left that medical science could do for her other than to see to her comfort.

You have to know that in Lillye's mind, she was carrying God's baby, hence her refusal to consider any toxic treatment that might affect the baby. As for the intimate connection that she felt with God, well, it was deeply personal and it was not to be questioned. In her mind, her faith in God's healing presence underscored her belief that God would intervene and that her health would be restored for the sake of the baby.

My heart still aches when I think about how Lillye's outlook changed from one of hope to one of despair. When she could no longer leave her bed because cancer had eaten away her hip bone; when her breast became an unrecognizable mound of malignant cells, and only then did she let go of the dream that she was to have God's baby. All of us had walked so carefully around her, trying not to interfere with her faith. And when the realization came to her that God's plan was not what she thought it would be, our hearts broke for her.

In her last few weeks, she kept a little spiral bound notebook by her bed and she began to write many notes to God. She would tear off each one and ask that it be taped to the walls in her room The notes contained all of her private supplications to God, and some bewildered questions for God. By then, she didn't care if we read them. To her they were a paper cocoon that allowed her sorrow to take form. The day she died we lovingly took each note down and put them all in the bed with her.

PSALM 43

1 Acquit me, God, and order my unfaithful thoughts. Absolve me from my transgressions. 2 You are my foundation. Why do my feet slip? Why is my gait unsteady when I walk on your path? 3 I search for divine understanding. I long to lift up my spirit to reach your enlightenment. 4 I want only to dwell in your consciousness; your joy gives me strength. I will sing songs of praise to you. 5 Why is my consciousness at such a low ebb? Why am I so uneasy? Although I falter I will keep seeking communion with my God.

Several sources I have read state that Psalm 43 is possibly the conclusion to number 42. There is repetition of language, and both have the theme of abandonment by God, followed by an expression of hope that God will once again be within reach.

I feel like both Psalm 42 and Psalm 43 encourage me to look beyond present circumstances and believe that God is simply one insight away from an understanding. As I read both psalms, I am asked to trust, to wait for the discernment that inevitably arrives when I practice sincere prayer and focused meditation.

The writer requests that God's Light and God's Truth show the way to the next right thing. I believe that to know God's light, I must understand the power that it has over darkness. I can travel on a path that can be overcome by darkness, so I can fully recognize the light. I must learn the difference between a self-imposed darkness, one caused by closing my eyes to Truth. Then there is the darkness that is inevitable, caused by being human and experiencing loss, with all its degrees of sorrow.

My best lessons are learned when I travel into a difficulty and attempt to understand it using the light of Truth. This is a sure way for me to learn what is important, and to examine the barriers that I have constructed to detour myself from my intended path. Reading through the psalms, I am given opportunities to absorb words from ancient others that remind me to be hopeful and wait for God.

PSALM 44

For the director of music. Of the Sons of Korah.[22]
A maskil.

1 I have read the ancient stories in your holy book, God; stories of your interventions with your faithful followers. 2 You gave them powers when they needed them; you helped them find the promised land, and they flourished. 3 It was their faith that gave them understanding; but it was your guidance that gave them strength and vigor. 4 God, when I feel the presence of spirit, I am inspired to do great things. 5 With prayer I can find a way through adversity; I am able to live within your truth. 6 I do not use negative words to hurt others, nor do I practice cruelty; 7 you show me the power of love at work in the world. 8 Because of that, I praise you and your love increases around me. 9 But there are still times when I cannot seem to find your wisdom; sometimes I feel alone without you. 10 I stumble on my path and you do not catch me. 11 I cannot hear that still small voice within me; those who support me

22 Sons of Korah: "Coldness and unproductiveness of life and good, because of one's not being willing to be guided in the love faculty...the barrenness (bald) of consciousness that result from dominance of the 'mind of the flesh'." Fillmore, Charles, *Metaphysical Bible Dictionary*, 392.

are gone. 12 I am given over to sorrow because I do not feel your presence. 13 My neighbors see my distress and ask me why I am saddened. 14 They do not understand my emptiness. 15 I am ashamed to be in their company. 16 I do not want their advice, for they do not feel as I do. 17 I pray that I have not brought this abandonment upon myself; I have tried to be true to your divine wisdom. 18 I believed that my heart was filled with your love, and I thought I was on a right path. 19 I do not want to let negative thoughts into my soul; I do not want to be in that darkness. 20 I must turn my mind away from error thinking for I do not like where these thoughts are leading me; 22 surely, God, you can see my distress. You know all my secrets. 23 God, my spirit needs to be awakened so that I can feel close to you again. 24 I can no longer hide my face from you and continue to give in to this misery. 25 I see now that I have too long relied on material things. I must rise above this place where I have put myself. 26 Let me be in communion with you so that I may feel your infinite love once again.

Psalm 44 leads me from the initial details of an awareness of God's amazing powers to a place where the writer feels abandoned. One turn of a phrase, and God seems to have disappeared. What was once reliable becomes questionable. Life can take an unexpected turn, and that is what comes to me in Psalm 44. Sometimes the change is gradual, barely noticeable as it is happening, until there comes a situation that cannot be ignored. Or perhaps a single incident triggers a cascade of changes, sometimes welcomed and sometimes horrifying.

The Bible is filled with stories of God as savior. God parts the seas, drops food from heaven, makes water flow in the driest desert, speaks to Moses from a burning bush. Despite these miracles, or maybe because of them, the writer is confounded about why there is no resolution available?

There are times when I forget that faith in God does not guarantee a problem-free existence. Psalm 44 reminds me God is both impermeable and transparent. Any faith commitment that I make will always be subject to my own doubt and misunderstanding. I forget that the big picture is beyond my grasp, that this is the impenetrable nature of God. Yet, in retrospect, I can gain an awareness of God's intervention. That is the message of hope and grace carried in the constancy of faith.

PSALM 45

For the director of music. To the tune of "Lillies". A maskil.

1 I consider carefully the words that I write as I study the world of the senses; I ask for wisdom when I speak of it. 2 In the eyes of many people, material wealth is a blessing from God. 3 Riches bring forth thoughts of great power; they can influence one to seek dominance over another. 4 But the people who are rich in spirit look for opportunities to support the causes of truth, mercy and justice. 5 They use their gifts for the betterment of people; they do not seek to control others. 6 They rely on the promise of justice; they seek the guidance of divine law to work harmoniously with others. 7 God blesses the righteous; the wicked will not benefit from the joy of God for their minds do not dwell in the realm of Spirit. 8 Spirit is eternal, bringing forth love; material substance will be used for the benefit of others. 9 The righteous will seek truth and their thoughts will be purified by the Christ Spirit. 10 The wise will honor creative ideas that lead to higher consciousness. 11 The spiritual person sees the beauty of creation all around. 12 The discerning person will enter sense consciousness with care and will not give in to false beliefs. 13 Purity of thought and action will be valued by the enlightened ones. 14 Spirit will be sought to refine the senses in the inner realm and in the outer world. 15 Gladness will cover the house of the righteous. 16 Its residents will know the difference between truth and error ways. 17 They will live and serve with joy and gladness.

Psalm 45 addresses the difference between an attraction to the material world for the sake of accumulating things, and the use of material things for the benefit of Creation.

It speaks of prosperity manifested and used for good purposes.

In her book, *How To Let God Help You*, Myrtle Fillmore writes about "The Law of Supply." This chapter pertains to the encouragement of Psalm 45 to use abundance in the service of good. She writes:

"You have some talent and capability that, used to the glory of God, and the honor of man, will bring you a rich reward. There is something that you can do better than anyone else can do it, and through the loving, efficient service you can render you will fulfill a need in this world. As you develop your inner resources and capabilities, the way is bound to open in the outer for you to 'cash in' on your talents.

We'll get at the prosperity consciousness now, and develop your inner spiritual resources and teach you to use them to supply whatever need arises. When you look with your all-seeing, all-discerning eye of faith, you see God's abundance manifesting to meet every need of yours. So practice seeing with this inner eye that beholds the eternal verities of Being. The more you exercise this eye, the better you will see with it."[23]

PSALM 46

For the director of music. Of the Sons of Korah. According to alamoth.[24] *A song.*

1 I reach for God's energy to give me strength of body, mind and spirit. 2 When fear approaches me I need only affirm that Spirit's presence will cast it out. 3 When negative thoughts plague me, I must aspire to a higher level of thought. 4 When I connect with Divine Mind I can find the cleansing power of God's love. 5 God is within me at all times, as close as my next breath. 6 I gather my thoughts and prepare to enter the silence where I can commune with God. 7 When I am there, I am inspired and strengthened. 8 I can see clearly the glory and power of God within me and around me. 9 God encourages me to live peacefully and harmoniously; God illuminates my thinking. 10 When I am in God's presence I am quiet and I believe in God's almighty power. 11 God is always with me; God is my fortress and my refuge.

For me, Psalm 46 is a perspective prayer, a reminder of my source, my protector, my fortress. I know that whatever happens, God is in the midst of it. Even when I am the mistress of my own mayhem, God is here. Whatever

---

23　Fillmore, Myrtle. *How To Let God Help You*, 143-144.

24　Alamoth: "An inner development, or soul progression." *Metaphysical Bible Dictionary*, 40.

drama I can concoct, God is available to help me change my point of view. When I am bustling around and ordering the universe to arrange things to my own liking, God is a reminder of where real power resides. No matter what happens, I can trust that God and Creation are in a rhythm that cannot be stopped or silenced. Even in the midst of dissonance, if I listen with an ear tuned to God, I will hear the music of the spheres.

PSALM 47

For the director of music. Of the Sons of Korah. A psalm.

1 Those who accomplish many things thank God for their abilities. 2 God is the source of all their awakenings; Spirit guides them wherever they go. 3 God gives us all the power of thought through which we manifest creative works. 4 God is with those who seek enlightenment and understanding. 5 To those who give thanks, God gives harmony and joy in return. 6 It is good to always praise God and God's creation. 7 The kingdom of God is within each of us: 8 There we can unite with Christ consciousness. 9 We can strengthen our faith and be guided by Spirit.

When I read Psalm 47 I am reminded of what is said in Micah 6:8. "And what does the Lord require of you? To act justly and to love mercy and to walk humbly with your God."

Following these simple precepts may not always be easy, but they are absolutely necessary if we are to have peace in our lives and our surroundings.

And, an attitude of gratitude is called for: one without reservations or conditions, one that clears the way to thinking and behaving in ways that honor thankfulness. Thoughts of abundance and prosperity come after grateful communion with God and Spirit. Then I am more likely to be open to receive the blessings that come my way, and to use them for good purposes.

PSALM 48

A song. A psalm of the Sons of Korah.

1 When we ascend in our consciousness to our most creative heights, we are filled with joy. 2 As we approach the loftiest plane of thought we are near to the highest wisdom and the clear light of truth. 4 With a sense of power, we feel entitled to that which is secret and hidden from us. 5 But the truth will only be ours when we are willing to forego error beliefs and false ideas. 6 Releasing error can be painful if we are not ready to do so. 7 But error is a harsh companion and its effects breed rigidity of thought. 8 Where many are gathered in God's temple, Spirit will bring understanding. 9 We come together to meditate on God's unfailing love. 10 We learn the ways of righteousness and justice, 11 and we come to praise God in the highest. 12 Holy thoughts reveal themselves as we spend time studying high ideals. 13 We are called to consider spiritual principles as guiding lights. 14 In these ways we can find God's unfailing love and presence.

Number 48 is a song of praise for the ability to find God within. But God exists all around us as well and I am encouraged to look for God's "unfailing love and presence" wherever I may find myself.

I have been so fortunate to have traveled and been in many places where I have felt the presence of God in all that surrounds me. There are destinations so holy to me that a visit becomes like a pilgrimage: the Sanctuario de Chimayo in New Mexico, the Grand Canyon, the ocean, are just a few examples. A pilgrimage is an opportunity to settle fully into the sacred works of creation, and to be blessed by the experience. The voyage itself is a time for an open spirit, and a time to welcome the anticipation of the wonders that await me.

For the writer of Psalm 48, God was to be found in an exalted place. Mount Zion was that place. The sacred Temple was built there and Mount Zion was a symbol of an impregnable, holy place. Regardless of what Mt. Zion stands for, what I read into this is that Zion can be found wherever God's creation is honored, revered, and cared for. Be that in a cathedral or in the slums, we are meant to recognize our fellow travelers as brothers and sisters; we are meant to be agents of kindness; we are meant to be caretakers of God's abundance.

PSALM 49

For the director of music. Of the Sons of Korah.[25]
A psalm.

1 Listen, for I will speak words of wisdom for those who live on earth, 2 no matter your station in life, or the number of your possessions. 3 I have meditated for a long time to reach this understanding. 4 I have read the holy books, I have sung songs of praise. 5 I have no fear of what is to come for I will resist the wicked – 6 those who trust only in material goods and speak loudly of their wealth. 7 When I reach spiritual consciousness, my body is strengthened. 8 No price can be put upon my life and earthly goods will stay behind me – 9 but even death will not separate me from spiritual truth. 10 Both the wise and the foolish will leave the earth; their possessions will stay behind. 11 My name may be engraved in a rock, but my spiritual essence will not diminish. 12 I know in my heart that no amount of riches will buy eternity on the earth plane. 13 Those who live only for the gathering of goods and do not search for Spirit will not know the joy of God's Divine Plan. 14 Even the most innocent among us will have to face an end to this familiar life. 15 But the living words of God are with us always and we will grow in spiritual power. 16 When riches hold more power than matters of spirit, although the temporal house may flourish, it must all be left behind. 17 Earthly splendor does not follow its owner when transition comes. 18

---

25   Korah: "Coldness and unproductiveness of life and good, because of one's not being willing to be guided in the love faculty (Korah was descended from Levi, who signifies the love faculty in individual consciousness) by the law of God." Fillmore, Charles, *Metaphysical Bible Dictionary*, 392.

People may mistake their possessions for blessings, but this prosperity is not of God. 19 While we are alive it is good to affirm the blessings of health and happiness and wisdom. 20 Wealth without truth is an empty comfort.

I mean no irreverence when I say that Psalm 49 is the Big Daddy of the, "You can't take it with you" psalms. It also addresses the great equalizer: no one escapes the death of the body regardless of financial status or social standing. It does not serve me to envy those who have "more" than I do because those thoughts distract me from my own spiritual purpose. None of my belongings will follow me beyond the ending of this life. In fact, I have learned as I get older that there comes a time to simplify, to downsize, so that I spend less time dusting and more time studying.

That being the case I am compelled to look at what I have and how I use it. This thinking goes beyond how big a check I can write to a particular cause. I am also called to use my time and energy in ways that serve my fellow travelers, and my corner of creation. I realize that intention is critical to the process of good works. It is right for me to examine my actions carefully and determine their true intent, to really look at the "why" of things. If I were to go on a pilgrimage, for example, it would be important for me to distinguish between checking off an item on a bucket list and the desire to grow spiritually from God's presence and grace along the way. Not just a personal gain for me, but an opportunity to do something with its best purpose in mind.

PSALM 50

A psalm of Asaph.[26]

1 There is nothing greater than Divine Mind, the creator of All That Is. 2 The laws of nature that govern the rising and setting of the sun, are of God. 3 God's presence will be felt throughout creation; God's words are the sum and substance of the ever-lasting cosmos. 4 With prayer and meditation the ideal and the manifest come together. 5 All children of God are included in the Divine invitation to live as one. 6 The unending love of God promotes the cause of justice for all. 7 Divine wisdom reveals itself to all who are truly listening and searching for it. 8 When consciousness is refined, the Kingdom of God is revealed in us. 9 God has no need for sacrificial offerings, 10 for all of Creation is of God. 11 God's love envelopes everything from the smallest creature to the mightiest blue whale. 12 Through the study of Divine Law, God offers spiritual sustenance. 13 Through God, mind and body are connected to Spirit. 14 For this we are to give thanks and affirm the power of God's presence. 15 We call on Spirit's mantle of peace in times of trouble and we are comforted, 16 but those who live by intellect alone live within a false consciousness. 17 They do not seek the truth that conquers error. 18 They are seduced by easy winnings and they live for misplaced power. 19 Their words are neither kind nor truthful. 20 They do not honor the rights of others. 21 They believe they are entitled to anything that they desire. They seek only material goods, and forsake the ways of Spirit. 22 They turn to God only when they are in need; they have no

---

26 Asaph is thought to be the musician/poet in charge of the temple worship services in King David's time.

intention of honoring God with their actions. 23 But those who give freely of their gifts will feel the joy of salvation.

With God there is awesome perfection, so pure that it is beyond my comprehension. In God's realm there is an orderliness that balances the tumult of creation with the stillness of peace. Beginnings and endings are in a constant dance, moving to a rhythm that God has ordained from the beginning.

As they study the universe, physicists discover smaller and smaller particles within atoms. Several years ago scientists were surmising that a subatomic particle, the Higgs Boson, might also be called, "the God particle", the basic building block of creation. I read the articles word for word but my brain is not big enough to understand the complexity of this microscopic grandeur that makes up an infinite creation.

For all of this, I am asked to give freely and gratefully. It's like paying it forward. What I receive comes to me through grace and must be given back with that same sense of grace and thanksgiving.

PSALM 51

For the director of music. A psalm of David. When the prophet Nathan came to him after David had committed adultery with Bathsheba.[27]

1 God, I come to you today with my head bowed, searching for forgiveness of my sins. 2 May Spirit bring your mercy and

---

27 Bathsheba: "As David united to Bath-sheba brought forth Solomon, so love in its fulfillment, or completion, establishes peace." *Metaphysical Bible Dictionary*, 99.

cleanse my thoughts of falsehoods. 3 I know very well when I have erred, and I cannot stop thinking of my transgressions. 4 My actions have been counter to what I know to be right; I am ashamed in your sight. 5 When you made me, God, I know that I was free from sin. 6 Your grace brought truth to me even before I was born. 7 Now I entreat you to wash me clean so that I can go forth with right thoughts. 8 Teach me your joy; put me back together with gladness. 9 Let me learn from you so that I may avoid false beliefs. 10 With you, I can be freed from worry and my spirit will go forth in kindness. 11 When I join in communion with you and with Holy Spirit, let me do so with love in my thoughts. 12 Restore in me a sense of right action; may I earnestly seek to do good. 13 May my actions be an example to others, and may I encourage others to seek you. 14 Where I have harmed others, God, I will make amends to them. 15 May I speak only words of kindness. 16 May I learn the value of giving to others when they are in need. 17 I will renounce self-serving thoughts and seek your truth instead. 18 I shall enter into the peace that exists in the silence, when I am in prayer or meditation. 19 I know of no greater comfort than to come to you with my spirit open to receive your grace.

Number 51 is a penitence prayer. Whenever I read it I remember times when, in my brokenness, I have had to seek forgiveness from God or from another human being. In many ways, this Psalm brings forth the Twelve Step wisdom of acknowledgment of wrongdoing and the courage to make amends when they are called for.

There have been many times when I have had to say I am sorry, God, for I have knowingly behaved in ways that are contrary to a clean life. I have transgressed, even when I knew it was wrong to do so. When I am floundering around in my own uncertainty, when I behave in ways that inevitably bring forth remorse, when I am following my own path of denial, I know by now what the result will be. Sometimes it is only in hindsight that I remember that I can always ask for direction and clarity ahead of time. When I look at consequences in the light of my contributions to them, only then am I able to take responsibility for what is mine.

What I need at these times is the courage to look at my behavior and review my choices before I make them. If I have acted in a hurtful way I must be willing to set things right. I pray that I may use the gift of free will in ways that promote kindness. If I seek out Divine Law for inspiration I can better live my life in ways that promote harmony where it is needed.

PSALM 52

For the director of music. A maskil of David. When Doeg the Edomite had gone to Saul and told him: "David has gone to the house of Ahimelek."[28]

1 Why do those who possess great power sometimes turn to wickedness? Why do they give great import to their words, the ones that contradict God's ways? 2 Those who live with untruths speak with sharp tongues. 3 They choose to live by error and false beliefs. 4 Their mouths speak only words of

---

28 According to the *Metaphysical Bible Dictionary*, Doeg represents "fearfulness, anxiety, timidity, in individual consciousness". (p. 176). At the same time, Ahimelek represents "A high ideal of intellectual consciousness that ministers to the religious thoughts of man." (p. 34) With these two contrasts in mind I understand a bit more about the context of the Psalm. David is searching for spiritual enlightenment in the midst of deception and treachery.

deception. 5 Surely there are consequences for such behaviors:
they have no foundation in God's truth; they come forth from
actions that are contrary to God's law. 6 Others can see them
for what they are, 7 and they will recognize those who sup-
port evil and destruction. 8 But I want only to be connected to
God's unfailing goodness; I know that the power of God's love
never fails me. 9 I will praise the gifts that come from God, for
I know they lead only to goodness.

Sometimes it helps my understanding of the meaning of a Psalm when I do a little research into the circumstances that may have prompted the prayer. The superscription of Psalm 52 says that it is a contemplative prayer of King David's. It may have been written during one of the many times of betrayal that David experienced in his lifetime.

When people grant themselves the power to do evil deeds, then evil itself becomes a little-g god. Like sin, evil can be seductive to those who crave what is not rightly theirs. There are degrees of evil, to be sure. Just for my own education I checked my iPhone dictionary only to find that there are at least 49 synonyms for evil. This is proof to me that we spend enough time thinking about it to have created many ways to express it.

The Revealing Word says evil is, "that which is not of God; unreality; error thought; a product of fallen human consciousness; negation. Evil is a parasite. It has no permanent life of itself; its whole existence depends on the life it borrows from its parent, and when the connection with the parent is severed nothing remains."[29]

---

29 Fillmore, Charles, *The Revealing Word*, 64.

What I do know for sure is that I have been given the gift of free will, that I always have a choice. I pray daily for the discernment to consciously choose what I know to be right, and in line with God's truth.

PSALM 53

For the director of music. According to mahalath.[30] *A maskil of David.*

1 The foolish ones do not acknowledge God. Their goodness is hidden behind evil behaviors; they do not seek redemption. 2 God cannot move through them because of their denials, and they do not honor divine principles. 3 They turn their faces from the light of God's love; there is not one among them who seeks harmony. 4 Why do they stifle their conscience? They reject any sustenance that comes from God; they never seek God's guidance. 5 But dread will come to them for they cannot find a place of comfort. Their thoughts are scattered around evil things; they do not feel shame for their actions. 6 If only restitution would come for them so that they would find the seed of truth! For God's holy vigor is available to all who seek it.

Psalm 53 is labelled as a teaching psalm by David. Written by a person of deep faith in God's enduring presence, the author labels non-believers as "foolish", and capable of egregious acts. Beyond that, it is hard to know who the subjects are and how the writer has come into contact with them.

---

30 Mahalath: "A peaceful, harmonious, light, rhythmically active and tuneful attitude of the soul, expressing on the carnal or human plane of soul consciousness, and also on a higher and more enlightened plane." *Metaphysical Bible Dictionary*, 416.

Perhaps the lesson is that at any time, I might join the rank of those fools. I know that I have contributed to mayhem in my life. What comes to me is the image of a slippery slope. I know the farther down I slide, the harder it is to climb back up to a higher standard. That's why, for me, it is essential to keep my face turned in God's direction.

We are all children of God. None are born with prejudice or hatred in their hearts. Love is the driving power of Creation. These beliefs are found throughout my spiritual resources and are spoken about and written about by wise and wonderful people. Psalm 53 draws attention to those whose actions run counter to the guiding principles of mercy and compassion. I suppose that the great challenge is to look beyond evil in search of understanding: what drives malevolence in one person and not another? How is one person able to commit murder, while another lives a life devoted to good works? I can never know the full measure of a life devoted to wrong actions. I cannot judge what I do not understand.

PSALM 54

For the director of music. With stringed instruments. A maskil of David. When the Ziphites[31] had gone to Saul and said, "Is not David hiding among us?"

1 I come to you, God, hoping for the redeeming strength of Spirit. 2 I enter the silence with thoughts of insecurity and fear. 3 I feel that I am under attack by those with whom I have no common bond – we do not agree on matters of spirit. 4 You are my guardian and my guide; you lead me on a righteous

---

31 Ziphites: "Thoughts belonging to the cleansing, purifying state of mind that Ziph signifies. The wilderness of Ziph signifies a lack of discipline, understanding, and cultivation in these thoughts." *Metaphysical Bible Dictionary*, 701.

path. 5 Let those who speak falsehoods about you cease to influence me. 6 Let my consciousness be refined; let me speak freely about your power and your love. 7 You have relieved my mind when it is troubled, and for that I will praise you always.

David was hiding from King Saul, who was out to get him. Saul was a king slipping into madness and paranoia and to him David was a threat. Psalm 54 represents another time when David prayed to God for protection from those who sought to do him harm.

I talk to God in my head and trust that what is born in my soul somehow reaches my Creator. I don't understand the physics of prayer. I wonder if such a petition travels at the speed of light, or if the rhythm of its sentiments is reconfigured into some divine language. David had every confidence in the power of his communication with God. He never hesitated to put his needs into a prayer. He asked for protection, for strength, for vindication, and, on occasion, for forgiveness.

It is hard for me sometimes to wait without being impatient, to trust without being a skeptic, to believe without being a doubter. I have come to the conclusion, however, that since I have the privilege of asking God for help or guidance, it's best if I'm courteous and attentive when I get an answer.

PSALM 55

For the director of music. With stringed instruments. A maskil of David.

1 I seek you, God, and I pray earnestly to you; 2 my hope is in your answer. My mind is not at peace; I am agitated. 3 I am aware of so much conflict around me, troubles that are not of my own making, that come from a place of anger. 4 My heart breaks when I see death and destruction in the world. 5 I am deeply affected by the sorrows and fears that plague others. 6 If I had freedom from the terrible distractions that surround me, I would be able to rest. 7 I would seek peaceful places, far away from conflict. 8 I would find shelter from disturbing thoughts and images. 9 God, where can you be found in the midst of such trouble? 10 It never ceases. Days and nights are filled with hateful acts. 11 I look around my city and I know that there are places where danger is the watchword. 12 If I were in the middle of such distress I would have no place to go but to you. 13 I turn to my friends for solace, 14 but they do not want to speak of such things. 15 All I can do is put aside thoughts of evil and enter into prayer with you. 16 I call to you, God, for wisdom and I know that I will find it. 17 You are with me always and I am free to seek you at any time of day or night. 18 Though I am deeply troubled, my time of prayer and meditation is filled with hopes of peace. 19 The power of God is eternal and God's protection is there for those who ask for it. 20 I observe those who act in ways that are contrary to God's teachings. 21 Their words are deceptive, and their actions are dangerous; they speak of wanting peace, but they are consumed with greed. 22 I will not be drawn in to such evil; I will keep my company with God and Divine Law and I will be safe from harm. 23 I will work for peace and justice because I trust in the goodness of God.

These days, finding chaos is as close as the next "breaking news" announcement on whatever media is active around me. Books and magazines are devoted to the tragedies happening around the world. Some of this sorrow takes place not that far from where I live. If I let myself do it, I can glue myself to a cable news channel until I've had my fill of controversy or destruction. The worst part is not knowing what to do as I witness the latest catastrophe.

In my life I have at times been a skilled escapist who lives with an aversion to chaos and disturbances. I can pull into my shell with the quickness of a startled turtle and choose to ride out the disorder until it subsides and nothing is required of me. As a good friend of mine says, I can go to a happy place until I think that it's safe to come back. The problem with this sort of avoidance tactic is that when I don't address the underlying issue, I should not be surprised when it rises up again.

Unity has taught me that prayer and meditation are far more useful than finding a cave to hide in. Whether it's a personal problem or a global issue, when I pray or meditate I find that, while the burden may not be removed, other possibilities for dealing with it will manifest. I can gain some perspective. I can get help to untangle my thoughts and I can discover a plan of action that is within my power and my capability.

PSALM 56

For the director of music. To the tune of "A Dove on Distant Oaks." Of David. A miktam. When the Philistines had seized him in Gath.[32]

1 God, I ask for your help to overcome thoughts that lead away from your goodness; my mind has been preoccupied with this for too long. 2 I fail to search for your divine ideas; my thoughts work against me. 3 I forget to affirm your presence and your power. 4 Yet, I know that through your Word you are revealed. What do I have to fear? 5 If I leave myself in error thinking I am led in ways that do not honor you. 6 My thoughts grow dark and I am unable to enter the mystery with you. 7 Let me instead enter into prayer with you; let me be open to your wisdom. 8 Your presence is within me and you know my deepest thoughts. 9 When I think in this way, my distress subsides and I feel your presence. 10 I can bring enlightened thoughts into my consciousness – 11 my trust in you is absolute. What do I have to fear? 12 I will offer myself to your scrutiny and I will give thanks for your guidance. 13 I will be in right relationship as I walk through my days.

Many of the Psalms make clear how David's connection to God is deeply personal. There are a whole series of lamentation prayers, prayers for

---

32   Gath: "A group of thoughts in the sense consciousness of man that believe in trial…, and look upon all experiences from the standpoint of seeming trial and suffering. Thus it causes the one who gives heed to it to become conscious of that which appears to be evil, when he should be busy seeing and believing in good only and thus coming into a consciousness of the blessing aspect of all his overcoming." *Metaphysical Bible Dictionary*, 224-225.

deliverance from pursuit, or capture, or devious plots that mean him harm. David asks what he has to fear, knowing that God is as close as his next breath.

Throughout my career as a nurse, I have come into contact with people experiencing great fear, for themselves or for a loved one. Wherever this occurs, it is a poignant call to action. I think about my experience as a nurse in a middle school, seeing children caught in the grip of fear, or desperation. Sometimes our resources were spread so thin there was not enough to meet the needs that presented themselves. Sometimes the best that I could offer was a peaceful space and an ear carefully tuned to what was not being said. Kindness, regardless of circumstances, was often the only good option. Advocacy, regardless of systemic barriers, is another valuable tactic. Compassion, regardless of my own fatigue, is called for under the circumstances.

Kindness, advocacy and compassion are not dependent upon money, or services, or policy and procedure manuals. They certainly do not always fix what needs fixing, but they are some of our most important responsibilities to one another, as fellow travelers. They can surely be augmented through the consistent practice of searching for the next right thing to do.

PSALM 57

For the director of music. To the tune of "Do Not Destroy." Of David. A miktam.[33] *When he had fled from Saul into the cave.*

1 I pray to you for peace to come within me, I come to you for relief from my unease. I meditate in your presence until my mind and spirit are calmed. 2 As I pray, I ask for your mercy. 3 Your divine wisdom is made clear — I must trust in your enduring love. 4 I will study your words and they will give me courage. My fears will be relieved and the actions of those who wish me ill will be directed away from me. 5 I listen for your voice and I am lifted up. 6 Other people speak of false beliefs and error — they see my distress. But I listen only for your counsel and I am set free. 7 Your love is ever present; my heart is lifted as in song. 8 My consciousness is tuned to Spirit's peace and I am raised up. 9 Wherever I am I will speak of my devotion to you. 10 Your love exists wherever there are stars in the universe. 11 Divine Mind is the source of all wisdom and your presence is like a mantle over the earth.

As I read Psalm 57 I think that surely its words have sustained people who did not always know if they would live to see another day, or who were prepared to be thrown in jail in the name of freedom, or who knew well that their bodies would be bruised and painful as a result of their actions. On one occasion when I was working with this psalm I happened to be reading about the Freedom Riders of the 1960's, and I have thought of

---

33 Miktam: "The entrance into consciousness of wise, inspiring, harmonious, uplifting thoughts of substance and Truth; and the inscribing of these Truth ideals in the memory." *Metaphysical Bible Dictionary*, 449.

their example whenever I encounter some of these Psalms. The Freedom Riders, non-violent in their behavior, withstood verbal taunts, blows from fists and batons, sprays of water from fire hoses, and people filled with venom. How often must they have said to each other the kind of goodbye's that go with the uncertainty of paths ever crossing again? And when they could, they sang holy hymns together from their jail cells.

I think also of one of my precious hospice patients, Sallie Mae. Sallie was in her late 90's when I met her. She had worked for decades ironing clothes with the precision of an engineer. She had battled her way through breast cancer until it got the better of her and she was mostly confined to bed, from which she could rise only with considerable pain and a lot of help. Sally had changed careers when she could no longer stand up to iron: she became a precision pray-er. She prayed for people she knew and for people she would never meet, halfway around the world and in need of divine intervention. Sally was old enough that she had lived through two world wars and the war at home against her African-American brethren, yet she always maintained a sweetness of spirit that can only come from a special relationship with God. I can't help but think that her prayers would have found a place among these psalms.

PSALM 58

For the director of music. To the tune of "Do Not Destroy." Of David. A miktam.

1 For you in power who do not govern with justice as your guide, why do you mistreat your people? 2 In your heads you create reasons to hand out punishments that are harsh and unfair. 3 From your beginning you were raised to bow down to evil and to curse God. 4 You spread error thinking before you, and no one can change you, 5 your ears are closed to God's Word. 6 Your words are as sharp as a lion's fangs, yet you lack real courage. 7 You live with negativity as your way of life; your judgment does not reflect God's truth. 8 Your darkness is not enough to hide your wickedness from the light of scrutiny. 9 Others will see you for what you are, and the power of true justice will sweep you away. 10 The innocents whom you have wounded will rejoice in your downfall. 11 When you are gone at last, a state of harmony will replace you and truth will prevail.

Psalm 58 is a harsh poem, calling out those who have turned away from a life of peace, those who live for violence and immediate gain. Through the ages, such people have endured. They exist in today's world. They live to inflict pain, to cause turmoil, and to take what is not theirs. They slaughter innocents. Their leaders conscript youngsters and teach them the ways of brutality by infiltrating their souls to replace kindness and compassion with the lull of "belonging" in a group. Evil then becomes a way of life.

We live in a world where our fellow travelers' pain is laid before us every day. The various sources of media communication inform me that there is unimaginable suffering that permeates the globe. From studying Unity teachings, I have reached an understanding that evil is free will gone awry. I believe that heinous acts can only happen when a person, for whatever reason, is cut off from knowledge of God's relentless pursuit of goodness.

When I have had enough of trying to understand corruption, of trying to set a context for violence, I turn to the Serenity Prayer: "God, grant me the serenity to accept the things I cannot change, the courage to change the things I can, and the wisdom to know the difference."

PSALM 59

For the director of music. To the tune of "Do Not Destroy." Of David. A miktam. When Saul had sent men to watch David's house in order to kill him.

1 If there are those who wish me ill, God, let me learn how to pray for them. 2 Remove their influence from my thinking and strengthen my will. 3 I do not understand their anger for I have done them no harm. 4 Even so, they are ready to cause me injury. I need your wisdom, God, for I am overwhelmed. 5 God, I have faith in the power of your truth; with it I can gain understanding and find a way through this unhappiness. 6 Even though my adversaries return, I do not have to join them. 7 There is no need for me to believe their harsh words. 8 I find my courage in communion with you. 9 You are my source of strength and security, 10 I know that you are always within me and that your presence watches over me. 11 I can withstand anything, knowing that your grace surrounds me. 12 Those who choose to live in the ways of error do not command me, 13 instead I send my prayers for them into the ether. 14 Though they may come around me, I will not be swayed by their wrong ideas. 15 I have all that I need to stave off adversity. 16 In the morning I will pray about your loving protection and know that I am secure in it. 17 I will seek your wisdom all day long and rely on your truth.

Psalm 59 is another of David's prayers to be delivered from danger. He makes the request with confidence, believing in his heart that he is the righteous one. God is known to champion the cause of justice and to side with the righteous, so it follows that David would assume that God is with him and for him!

Compared to David's issues, mine are much less complicated. I don't have enemies seeking to end my life; I don't have a royal legacy to strive for; I am not in charge of a whole people. Nevertheless, I have had occasions when I find myself in the midst of a controversy. At those times it is empowering to remember that prayer will help me to clarify what my part is in creating the situation.

Then, I have the option of acknowledging my contribution and doing what I can to fix whatever wrong I may have committed. Once I have done that I am much more likely to find a way to coexist while honoring our differences. I do not need to fear our dissimilarities. Instead I can look for the wisdom they impart.

PSALM 60

For the director of music. To the tune of "The Lily of the Covenant." A miktam of David. For teaching. When he fought Aram Naharaim and Aram Zobah, and when Joab returned and struck down twelve thousand Edomites in the Valley of Salt.

1 We have limited our thoughts to inferior ones that do not honor your truth; we have felt what we thought was your wrath, God. 2 Your transformation happens around us and we do not recognize it. 3 We have felt the sorrow of alienation; we have searched for your living water. 4 But when we move beyond thoughts of material gain, we come closer to your wisdom. 5 We are learning to love and to stop honoring our imperfect thoughts. 6 We seek your Word so that we may walk upright in your light and abide as spiritual beings. 7 We seek a higher consciousness and better understanding; through our affirmations we will raise our ideals. 8 Your thoughts are only of goodness; you teach us to honor our physical bodies and to train our senses to seek your good. 9 You will show us the spiritual center of our consciousness. 10 God, you will never turn against us for you come from the place of purest love. 11 We seek your wisdom to raise us from our limited sense consciousness. 12 Through you we will attain spiritual discipline and enlightenment.

I think of Psalm 60 as a song written to God, asking for enlightenment in a time of great uncertainty. It takes some painfully honest self-reflection to evaluate my part whenever I have created my own mess. I would prefer to avoid that discomfort, but Unity teaches me that I am better off praying for clarity. I must be willing to accept the next steps that are necessary to undo what I have wrought.

I believe God does not meddle in my affairs. Instead, I have been gifted with free will and the ability to make choices. In Unity teachings, free will is defined as follows: "Man's inherent freedom to act as he determines. There can be no perfect expression without perfect freedom of will. If man determines to act in accord with divine law, he builds harmony, health, happiness, and eternal life, which is heaven."[34]

I like to believe that I possess a certain amount of intelligence and common sense. Given enough time and patience I can usually reason out an

34 Fillmore, Charles, *The Revealing Word*, 79.

answer or a solution. But,I have been put in my place a time or two. A good example of this is when my daughter and I visited an exhibit of Albert Einstein's work. We got our tickets with great anticipation, poised to look at the work of one of the greatest minds in history. However, about two rooms into the exhibit it was evident to both of us that we were in way over our heads. I remember casually sneaking out of the building hoping that I didn't look as dumb as I felt.

Sometimes, trying to put together a coherent thought about God's nature is like being locked in the Einstein exhibit. I see letters and numbers that I recognize individually, but I'll be darned if I can decipher them when they are strung together. Then I remember that I am simply asked to do God's work with a sense of purpose. I am to have faith that God has given me what I need to see a problem simply as a solution waiting to be discovered.

PSALM 61

For the director of music. With stringed instruments. Of David.

1 I have entered the silence searching for you, God. 2 I have examined my heart and not found you; I need your counsel in order to ease my mind. 3 I know that with you and with Spirit I find peace, and my faith is strengthened. 4 Because of you I have put on this body and my spirit is forever secure in you. 5 God, when I pray I ask that your truth be revealed to me; I will follow your goodness in all of my actions. 6 When I am directed by Spirit I am at my best and my life is enriched. 7 I know that eternal love and faithfulness are from you; your will for me is perfection of body, mind and spirit. 8 As I praise

*you, my troubled mind is eased and I will go through my days
with confidence.*

Psalm 61 speaks to me about the power of prayer. When I give a prayer over
to God I open heart and soul to God's limitless possibilities. I acknowledge
God's energy in the realm of Creation. I remember that I am an integral
part of God's plan. When I compose a prayer there is an opportunity to
reflect carefully on what I am really asking for. I must be clear about what
I am attempting to do. I also know that my request, sometimes an urgent
entreaty, is simply a reflection of how I hope things will be, knowing that
guarantees don't come automatically.

Sometimes I must judge whether my prayers are my complaints, or my
wishful thinking, or my selfish longings. I know that I have sent out prayers
that make very little sense, coming as they do from a place of fear and confusion. There are times when I don't really know what I need, I just don't
want this _____. (Fill in the blank.).

My part in the covenant of prayer is to honor the vows I have made to God
by thinking carefully about what I'm requesting. I pray for good outcomes
for myself and others, wanting to include my best hopes in the equation. I
pray for the wisdom to care for my corner of creation. I pray that I will act
with kindness and respect toward others. And, I believe that when I pray
carefully and mindfully, I do so in the shadow of God's great mystery, and
in the care of God's great love.

PSALM 62

For the director of music. For Jeduthun.[35] *A psalm of David.*

1 When my soul is worn and tired, I seek God's peace; I am restored because of it. 2 I do not doubt that God's energy is the source of my strength; because of it I cannot be brought down. 3 Though adversaries may rise against me I can meet them with kindness and an open mind. 4 No matter their intentions I am able to see the Christ in them; I do not let their words hurt me. 5 I ask God for patience and I am composed. 6 I trust that with God's support I will be able to find a solution. 7 God's divine law teaches me to behave honorably, no matter the circumstance. 8 I know that I can enter the silence when I am distressed and pray for guidance. 9 If there is any wickedness around me I will choose the higher path. 10 I do not trust in empty words and gestures; I am not fooled when riches take the place of integrity. 11 In the silence I have heard God's powerful words, 12 encouraging me to act with love and fairness towards all.

From God comes salvation, deliverance and any sense of an honorable life. One way I learn this is to be open to and aware of the God-moments that happen every day. On those days when I don't bother to look for these gems, my life is not as rich as it can be. When I divert my focus from God, I miss these opportunities. Some God-moments are tiny and precious and

---

35　Jeduthun: "The spirit of love, joy, and praise vibrating exultantly through the whole spiritual consciousness of man, and playing on every center in his organism, establishing divine harmony (*full of songs of praise, praising, lauding, love's celebration*)." *Metaphysical Bible Dictionary*, 327.

easily missed. Some are huge and joyous. Some are just plain funny and call forth that most healing of gifts that is laughter. Some carry messages, sometimes painful, but always wrapped around an important teaching.

Honoring these moments leads me to a life of substance, not defined by wealth or station in life. I can measure carefully what I have to offer, and give away only what will benefit my fellow traveler. I have learned that giving of any kind is best done without the coloring of my own assumptions as a part of the gift. When I am engaged in giving to another, I am wise to remember this 12 Step wisdom: "Take what you like, and leave the rest."

PSALM 63

A psalm of David. When he was in the Desert of Judah

1 God, my God, I search for you; I am in a dry place, even tears don't flow from my eyes. I thirst for your living water. 2 I have been with you in the quiet places where we meet, and my mind has felt your holiness. 3 It is your love that built the universe, star by star. 4 I will speak about your glory and I will lift my consciousness to you. 5 From you, God, comes all of my abundance; I have everything I need. 6 Through the longest nights you are with me. 7 I rely on your grace and I sing of your goodness. 8 I depend on you and I am open to your truth. 9 If any ill befalls me I enter into prayer and meditation with you. 10 I will not fear evil because you do not give it any power. 11 My life is guided by Spirit and I will live my life according to your truth.

I love the hopeful tone of Psalm 63, and the reminder of all the places where God is to be found. I think about how often God has intervened on my behalf; I consider that there have been intercessions beyond my awareness that have lifted my unknowing self from harm. I am reminded again of the importance of conscious gratitude for all the blessings, seen and unseen, that have shaped my life. Because of them, I have become so aware of the eternal power of grace. It runs as a current that sustains creation and gives substance to its fabric. God's grace is always available.

I have mentioned the "God Particle," the Higgs Boson, discovered a few years ago by particle physicists. I have since learned there is another discovery, another piece of creation's building blocks, called a "Gluon." As the name implies, Gluons help to hold matter together, thereby holding us together. Grace or Gluons, they're really the same thing.

PSALM 64

For the director of music. A psalm of David.

1 Today, God, I need your counsel; I am surrounded by negative thoughts. 2 I have no desire to be a part of the discord around me. 3 People speak unkind words to each other and about each other. 4 Their rancor is aimed at anyone with whom they disagree. 5 They gather together to speak ill of people; they say "Who will stop us?" 6 They agree on ways that will undermine the efforts of others; their methods are not sincere. 7 God, I pray for clarity so that I will not be taken in by their malice. 8 My desire is to have an attitude of calmness and justice as I interact with them. 9 I pray that I may find your words of wisdom to use when I am in their presence. 10 May I live in a state of harmony so that your truth will guide my actions towards them.

Anyone who has managed to escape the erosion of spirit that occurs when disagreement and discord reign is fortunate indeed. These situations are uncomfortable and unproductive. In my career I have encountered the corrosive nature of actions that serve no useful purpose, actions that simply add to the negative energy rather than contribute to any useful solution.

I would not always have thought to pray about my place in such doings. After a particularly agonizing meeting, a coworker and I were leaving the hospital. We were both frustrated by the lack of productive participation and the negative nature of the meeting. Suddenly she stopped outside of the chapel in the hospital lobby and invited me to go in with her to pray. I must have looked at her as if she had two heads and all she said was, "What can it hurt?"

The result of that brief sojourn in the chapel was a very helpful change in my own attitude. Since then I have entered the silence with the purpose of asking for clarity when faced with such a situation. I ask for guidance to be able to stand up for my principles, to practice kindness, and to seek to understand where another person might be coming from. I ask for the ability to hold my tongue when I have nothing of real value to offer. I ask for the courage to behave in ways that honor peaceful resolution.

This practice has made all the difference for me.

PSALM 65

For the director of music. A psalm of David. A song.

1 When praise to God prevails, abundance is manifested. 2 God gives back to all who enter into this communion. 3 When time is spent with God, error thinking is changed into thoughts of

*good. 4 Those who encounter God are richly blessed and filled
with goodness. 5 Peace and satisfaction come to those who
seek God throughout the earth, 6 for God is omnipresent no
matter where God is sought. 7 God is the universal Mind from
which all ideas come forth. 8 By day or by night, God's awesome powers are the source of joy and wonder. 9 God's all pro-
viding law turns seeds into plants for food; God's streams of
living water bring the land to life. 10 God's blessing multiplies
the crops; gentle rains soak the earth. 11 The hands of those
who work the fields produce an abundance of nourishment. 12
Pastures thrive, the fields are green with new life. 13 Thoughts
of plenty abound, gratitude predominates, and the hills are
clothed in prosperity.*

Psalm 65 is an eloquent reminder of the bounty that comes from working in
concert with God who is the Source, the Creator, our Mother/Father presence. From that moment billions of years ago, when Divine Mind blew a
universe into existence, our Creator has been moving carefully through the
vastness, bringing forth the incredible power of a tiny seed that becomes
a sturdy tree. Looking at the riot of green outside of my Florida window I
feel a connection with each living thing.

Studying God's creation is like watching the Discovery Channel or a
National Geographic special program. There is always something new
to learn through astounding insights into the elegance of God's designs.
Crops and flocks, creatures living in the deepest parts of the sea, the intelligence of dolphins, the sculpting powers of wind and water, the miracle of
birth. And further removed from this world are black holes, dark matter,
supernovas, clouds of stars, the vastness of galaxies.

There is some comfort in knowing that even Albert Einstein was sometimes perplexed by the wonders of God's endless possibilities.

PSALM 66

For the director of music. A song. A psalm.

1 Sing for joy to God and to Spirit. 2 The wonders of this world awaken us to God's goodness. 3 God's creation reveals itself as holy substance takes form in the universe. 4 Our very bodies are made from the same matter that makes up the stars. 5 When we open our eyes and take in God's works we are filled with awe. 6 God magnifies the universal life force so that our energy is fully manifested. 7 All things are possible with God. 8 We celebrate the gifts that come from God, and we lift our voices in praise; 9 we seek to do good works in return. 10 Through prayer and meditation our thoughts can be refined like purest silver. 11 When we are prisoners of our thoughts, prayer can set us free. 12 When we dwell too long in error thinking, meditation can cleanse our senses. 13 We raise our consciousness when we turn ourselves over to God. 14 God is the presence that ensures our safety. 15 We bring our gifts before God to receive God's blessing and we use our gifts for good. 16 We will speak of God's grace so that others may know of God's bounty. 17 We will listen for the inner voices that guide us to Spirit. 18 We will learn from our mistakes by entering the silence, 19 and asking what their lessons might be. 20 We will rest within the assurance of God's unending love.

Psalm 66 is a praise psalm from its opening to its last verses. Unity's co-founder, Charles Fillmore, defines praise as follows:

"The purpose of praise is to awaken in ourselves a higher realization of the omnipresence and power of God. Prayer and praise change man, not God. The mental attitude that praise sets up stimulates, quickens, whirls into action, and finally establishes in character the ideals of which they are the vehicle."

"Through an inherent law of mind action we increase whatever we praise. The whole creation responds to praise, and is glad. Animals and children quickly respond to praise. One can praise a weak body into strength, a fearful heart into peace and trust, shattered nerves into poise and power, a failing business into prosperity and success, want and insufficiency into supply and support."[36]

The other theme that comes through to me in Psalm 66 is that of redemption. In this matter I can't speak for anyone but myself. Redemption, and the hope for it, comes through the personal covenant that I share with God. It is a powerful spiritual cleanser achieved one small step at a time. It is a daily endeavor, lived out through kindness and compassion in both thought and behavior. Some days I don't even come close to earning that merit badge, but I have learned that mending my mistakes counts toward making proper amends. Doing so when it is called for makes me a better human being.

---

36   Fillmore, Charles, *The Revealing Word*, 152.

PSALM 67

For the director of music. With stringed instruments. A psalm. A song.

1 God showers grace upon us and gives us spiritual enlightenment – 2 so that we may praise God's ways with words and songs. God's redemption frees us from limitations of thought. 3 When we tell of God's abundance we teach others about God's omnipresence. 4 When we share our thoughts with God we increase our spiritual powers. 5 We learn the value of true gratitude; we learn the importance of devotion to God. 6 Our work is fruitful and honors God; in return, we are blessed. 7 Others will see the result of our dedication, and they will also approach God with awe and reverence.

In my waking hours I have plenty of time to praise God and be grateful be it through prayer and reflection, or through action and intention. An act of kindness is a prayer; work with a purpose is a meditation; fruitful conversation is an intention; healthy self-care is gratitude at work. God is present in all of these occasions, and it's up to me to remember that.

Unity teaches me that to praise God means to acknowledge God within, and to courageously enter into the silence, where the greatest lessons are learned. I praise God when I search for the good in myself and in someone else. I praise God when I seek to change my negative thinking into affirmations of faith. When I am true to my commitments, I honor promises made to God. And, when I am a tender caregiver of creation, I am praising God with all I have to give.

PSALM 68

For the director of music. Of David. A psalm. A song.

1 When in a time of trouble, it is good to call upon God for help. 2 In God's presence, wrong thinking dissipates – the breath of Spirit cleanses our thoughts. 3 Those who align their soul with God's love will find peace and joy. 4 Singing praises to God raises our consciousness and restores harmony within. 5 God guides us when we have forgotten about God's abundance. 6 When we are prisoners of our own thoughts, we find release through prayer and meditation. 7 When our thoughts stray far beyond our own truth, 8 we have only to seek God within and we will be freed from turmoil. 9 God's love brings refreshed ideas to us when we are open to them. 10 There is no poverty of spirit when in God's presence. 11 God's words speak to us of plenty when we feel impoverished. 12 If we are guided by Spirit, we have nothing to fear. 13 When we are tempted to stray from God's goodness, Spirit moves us to study divine law. 14 While in the shadows, we are given enlightenment. 15 Our understanding grows as we study divine substance; 16 and learn of the living energy that creates all things. 17 When we enter the sanctuary of our soul we are closest to God. 18 Our consciousness will be elevated and we will be set free from doubt. 19 We praise your loving ways and seek to follow them each day. 20 When we correct our error thinking we are freed from limitations, including thoughts of death. 21 We will keep company with those who also seek God's wisdom. 22 Our work will be of benefit to others, 23 and we will base it on spiritual principles. 24 We will walk humbly with our God and with our fellow travelers. 25 Songs of praise will fill our hearts, and words of welcome will fill our mouths. 26 When we are in the sanctuary we will sing with joy. 27 Our faith increases beyond what we have known before; our thoughts are cleansed and purified. 28 Our powers increase as we use our faculties for good. 29 We will receive the gift of peace. 30 Our unruly thoughts will not possess us as we enter into the silence. 31 Instead, they will be brought from obscurity into the light of scrutiny. 32 We will be grateful in God's presence, 33 as we are raised to a new level of spiritual conscious-ness. 34 In the presence of high ideals we will think positive thoughts. 35 Our minds will be sources of transformation. We will always praise God.

Psalm 68 could have been written by anyone seeking to live a life of service to God. Throughout the verses I find the encouragement to go within to that place where God and I meet. Once there, I open my mind to God's endless possibilities. I pray that my thinking will be elevated to a higher plane so that new and creative ideas can come to me. These ideas are the building blocks of my best life and all I have to do is let them into my consciousness!

I read a version of this psalm a few months before I retired from a long career in nursing. What came to me was that I needed to start thinking about what would replace my 40+ hour work week. It had not occurred to me that I would ever have such a large amount of discretionary time on my hands. To be honest, that thought filled me with the uneasy stirrings of anxiety.

The morning that I read this particular psalm was the beginning of my journey inward to seek God's guidance for the coming months. As I visual-ized myself without a schedule to follow, I prayed to God for enlightenment as to my options. In this process I realized that, while I was ready to retire from nursing, I was not ready to retire from a productive life. Gradually, in times of prayer and meditation, I began to imagine different uses of my time and my experience.

Without that focused time spent with God and Spirit I don't know how long I would have floundered through my days. As it is, a whole new direction opened up for me and I was able to start a second career. This is the gift that comes with discernment, with patience, and with prayer and meditation.

PSALM 69

For the director of music. To the tune of "Lilies." Of David.

1 Today, God, I am in distress. I feel as though I am engulfed in troubled waters. 2 I can find no foothold on which to anchor myself. 3 I know how I have gotten in to this dire situation, but I must seek your counsel for the way to remove myself. 4 I cannot depend on those around me for help, for they have nothing to give me. 5 I can see where I have erred, and I bring this to you so that I may be enlightened. 6 I do not want to set such an example for others; I must examine my actions and find my responsibility. 7 My transgressions are mine alone, you have no part in them. 8 Because I have brought this on myself, I do not turn to others for relief. 9 I want to be free from these bonds lest anyone think that you have placed them on me. 10 I must meditate on truth and give up my error thinking. 11 When I grieve over what I have done I must bring it to you in the silence. 12 Your wisdom can help me see the road ahead that leads to redemption. 13 I pray that I will follow the path that leads to you. 14 I will use your strength to lift myself up from the depths. 15 I know with certainty that your grace surrounds me while I rise up in search of you. 16 Your words will come to me when I ask for your help. 17 I do not have to wait long in the silence before you remind me that your love is always in me and around me. 18 You are as close as my next breath. 19 You know the depth of my shame and what I have done to cause it. 20 Though I may be tempted to look for sympathy from others, I must abide with you and ask for Spirit to surround me with forgiveness. 21 I must learn to forgive myself and not dwell in bitterness. 22 I must be awakened to a new way of approaching challenges so that I do not fall into this trap again. 23 May I learn to walk upright without bowing to false thoughts. 24 May I find higher thoughts and, with them, find the blessing. 25 May I walk away from places that are not of benefit to anyone. 26 May I ask to be forgiven if I have caused hurt to another being. 27 I do not want to repeat my errors. 28 If I do so, may I learn a bitter lesson that will teach me once and for all. 29 When I am tempted by error thinking I ask for your protection. 30 I will be grateful for any intervention that leads to right action. 31 I will devote myself to your healing ways. 32 I will join with those who seek to improve personal consciousness. 33 I bring my cares to you, and with prayer and meditation I see my next steps. 34 God, you are above and beneath me, in front of me and behind me. 35 I know where to go for peace and resolution; 36 may I return to that place where Spirit dwells with me.

Psalm 69 is also a prayer of deep longing for release from a difficult turn of circumstances. I have been in such a place of fear and rumination, not fully convinced that I would be set free from my shadow land. When I reached out to God, it was with a whisper, barely audible to me. I could not search too far outside of my head, nor could I think of any moment but the one that I was stuck in. For the author of Psalm 69, the fear and sorrow came from deep within. That is a kind of wilderness in which my soul finds itself wandering. This is my human condition sometimes: perplexed, subject to hopelessness, and unclear as to my next steps. In my sorrow, I forget to ask for direction until the only thing that I am sure of is that I am lost.

Unity has taught me that these are the times when I need to be quiet and listen and wait for a direction to come to me. It involves spiritual discipline in that I must commit to myself that I will enter the silence with God and Spirit. Once there I can repeat the assurance God is with me and I am loved and protected, sometimes from myself.

PSALM 70

For the director of music. Of David. A petition.

1 I ask for your help to come now, God, for I am deeply troubled. 2 I do not want to give in to my fears, for they are in the way of my prayers for relief. I need your strength to turn and face my disquiet. 3 Only then can I dissolve the bonds of negativity that hold me back. 4 I know in my heart that the power to overcome my distress is within me, that what I most need to do is to be in a quiet place and reflect on your love. 5 My spirit is at a low ebb; I need to open myself to your energy and listen for your wisdom. I pray for release from my despair to come quickly.

This is an impatient prayer, one I have certainly said at times. I wonder why I am asking for God's immediate attention? What I know for sure is that God is no further from me than the air that sustains my life. Then I remember it is not God who keeps me bound to my fear. That state of being, unsettling as it is, wells up in me when I give in to doubt that there is no answer to be had. It denotes a laziness of spirit, or an excuse to neglect my responsibilities. It is me looking for a quick fix.

Sometimes I wonder what gives me the right to demand anything from God, especially if my distress is of my own making. Perhaps I have made an uninformed choice whose outcome is troublesome; maybe I have chosen an easier, softer way that has led to a dead end; perhaps I have kept quiet when, in good conscience, I should have spoken up.

When I do a thorough soul searching I sometimes end up in the Land of Oz, where I have become the cowardly lion, the rigid tin man, and the brainless scarecrow, all in one. Instead of relying on tried and true prayer and meditation I depend upon the man behind the curtain who offers nothing but illusions and false claims.

PSALM 71

1 God, I come to you for help; my thoughts are disturbed. 2 I need to study your truth and turn my thinking in positive directions. 3 In the silence there is a shelter that is always available to me; it is where I go when I need to feel close to you and to Spirit. 4 I turn to you when my consciousness is overcome by error thoughts; when I have forgotten the power of denials. 5 I have relied on your wisdom since my youth. 6 You brought me safely into this life; for that I give thanks. 7 I live my life according to your teachings so that I may be an example to others. 8 I use my words carefully so they may reflect my love for you. 9 I know that you are with me throughout my days; my strength will always come from you. 10 If anyone speaks against me, I endeavor to understand why. 11 I come to you for a deeper understanding of my next steps when I am faced with conflict. 12 I know that you are as close as my next breath. 13 When I am tempted by materiality I will pray for the cleansing truth of Spirit. 14 I will remember the gifts of spiritual discernment when I am in doubt. 15 I will meditate on your vast creation and speak of your miracles, though I do not understand them all. 16 Your power throughout the universe cannot be adequately explained. 17 No matter my age, there is always more for me to learn about your love. 18 May I continue to speak of your love until the end of my days. 19 Your harmony vibrates throughout the heavens and your works are too many to speak of. 20 In my lifetime I have experienced difficulty, but studying your wisdom brings resolution and peace. 21 Spirit brings me comfort and I am lifted up. 22 When I can, I sing about your marvelous ways. 23 I will tell all about your restoring powers. 24 I will continue to study your lessons and speak of your goodness.

I have appreciated reading Myrtle Fillmore's book, *How To Let God Help You*. As I read through this psalm I make a connection with a chapter from this book called, "The Mind Receives," especially the following paragraphs:

"As you study, you will learn that your mind receives from two sources: the Universal Mind of Being, which has at its outlet through your consciousness, and the intellectual activities of the individual minds about you, which are both conscious and subconscious phases of expression.

"Now, that which you receive from the Mind of God is always good, always helpful, health-inspiring and peace-inspiring. That which you receive from the reports of your senses, or the minds of others, may be true and helpful or it may be false and harmful.

"The study and practice of Truth will help you to discriminate between the false and the true, and to combine rightly the ideas of the Christ Mind within you, that you may express and bring forth whatsoever you will."[37]

PSALM 72

Of Solomon.

1 May the leader govern with integrity and be guided by truth. 2 May all people be treated with dignity and fairness. 3 It is right that leaders work for abundance for all, so that prosperity will come to everyone. 4 As evidence of injustice surfaces, may the leader seek God's guidance and work for the benefit of all. 5 May the ruler be guided by Spirit's light, and by the power of intelligence. 6 May the leader's ideas produce growth, like a fertile field watered by gentle rains. 7 As long as the leader governs may the light of understanding and wisdom prevail. 8 As the leader rules with equity, may this influence grow. 9 During challenging times, may the leader not bow to the influence of false beliefs. 10 During hard times, may the ruler find wholeness for all. 11 Others will be respectful and seek the

---

37   Fillmore, Myrtle, *How To Let God Help You*, 54.

leader's counsel. 12 It is widely known that the leader will help those in need, and those who have nowhere to live. 13 Those who are in great need will go to the leader and receive help. 14 From a place of goodness, the one in authority will provide protection for the oppressed. 15 The leader will receive gifts of the spirit and the prayers of the people. 16 May abundance come for all people. 17 Under the leader's guidance, may the people experience growth. 18 The just leader will be praised and perceived to have great wisdom. 19 May the leader's name be remembered for good works. Amen. 20 This concludes the prayers of the one who represents Divine Love.

In ancient Israel, the King was considered to be God's representative on earth. Psalm 72 is said to be "of Solomon," and it is mostly an illustration of the benefits of a just and caring ruler. The leader is to be concerned with the needs of the poor and the oppressed. The leader is the defender of those caught in the mire of poverty and injustice.

Reflecting on this psalm, I think that a ruler's effectiveness is partly a result of the collective will of the people. All of the qualities of a fair and just ruler should be lived out in individual lives as well. I am also called to work on behalf of the needy, to object to oppression and injustice, to use my abilities for the betterment of my corner of creation.

Chapter Four

BOOK III
Psalms 73–89

PSALM 73

A psalm of Asaph.

1 God's goodness is available to those who understand the divine nature of the body. 2 But I myself had lost my perspective and slipped into thoughts of lack. 3 My judgment was skewed and my thoughts strayed to desire for the material gain that others had achieved. 4 I thought of them as more fortunate than I, with greater riches and better health. 5 I was tempted by their false claims of quick prosperity and promises of easy wealth. 6 Their vanity had gotten the better of them, their thoughts turned to greed. 7 Their hearts were hardened to the truth; they imagined only iniquity. 8 Their words were not based in truth, they had no respect for others who were different from them. 9 They spoke as owners of the kingdom of God, but their thoughts were bound to sense consciousness. 10 Their followers took in their words and believed in their negative announcements. 11 They gave no thought to God within them and did not seek God at all. 12 Their possessions became as gods to them. 13 I was troubled by all of this and sought to free myself from their allure. 14 Although I prayed earnestly for release, each day I had to begin my prayers anew. 15 I meditated on the source of my temptation. 16 I asked God and Spirit to cleanse my thinking 17 so that I could change the direction of my path. 18 I understood that such an attachment to wealth and possessions would lead me in a wrong direction. 19 I understood how quickly possessions can be stripped away, leaving an empty heart to mourn them. 20 Dreams of fame and fortune dissipate with the morning light. 21 At first my heart felt great sadness. I gave in to thoughts of deprivation, 22 and I felt pity for myself. 23 I turned my thinking to you, God, and I went to the quiet place where you are always found. 24 I prayed for guidance and I felt the presence of Spirit. 25 When I meditated on your abundant love I realized that richness of Spirit is what I must seek. 26 Though material possessions surround me, they are not my owners. 27 With you, I have everything I need and I can affirm the bounties of creation. 28 I remember that the kingdom is within me. With your love, God, I am enriched beyond measure.

Psalm 73 always speaks to me. It reminds me that envy and greed are my shadow sides. When I live in their gloom, I give away my self-confidence and spend time longing to be thin and wealthy. "In my next life," I say. This is how I diminish my own life, the only one available to me at the moment. This is how I disown the richness of my life experiences and the abundance that I now enjoy. Psalm 73 serves as a mirror to me and as much as I want to avoid looking in it, I can't escape its truth.

This psalm is attributed to Asaph, a man who served in the courts of King David and King Solomon. To me, his writing shows that he gained insight to see that envy and thoughts of lack are heavy burdens capable of distorting wisdom and truth. He realized that he was discounting his own life, making it seem small and unimportant because he envied what others had. Most of all, he was forgetting how his relationship with God brought him all that he really needed.

Sometimes I do battle with a little-g god I call, "Not enough." When I pray about this state of mind I recognize my dark side, dipped in self-pity, with a coating of resentment. This tendency can drag me under until I remember to ask God for forgiveness when I have lapsed into this kind of thinking.

As I am praying, I ask for insight. I ask for the truth to be laid out before me and that my eyes be open to see it. There is no safer place for me to be than to be in relationship with my Creator when I am struggling with my mundane worries.

PSALM 74

A maskil of Asaph.

1 God, I turn to you now because I am in a place of anger and I am not sure of its source. 2 I wish to lift my thoughts above such a dark place and find relief. 3 Yet, I persist in allowing my will to turn me in a wrong direction. 4 Angry thoughts are signs of my discontent. 5 I resist with my will all attempts to connect with your life-giving truth. 6 I cause damage to my body, mind, and soul when I am outside of wisdom consciousness. 7 I resist the cleansing that comes with Spirit's purifying fire, 8 and I persist in my limited thinking. 9 I look for a way through this and I long to know how long I will feel this way. 10 How long will I stay in this place? How long will I hold this anger in my thoughts? 11 Why can't I find a place of love and kindness in which to dwell? 12 God, I pray that I may know your redemptive power. 13 You are the source of truth and peace, if only I would turn over my stubborn will. 14 I know that in the silence, with you, I will surely find resolution. 15 I will find your streams of living water that will quench this outrage that I feel. 6 I must seek you day and night, and not give in to my selfishness. 17 You are the passion that builds Creation; how can I forsake that love? 18 While others persist in fury, I must stop giving in to their influence. 19 When I stay with them, all possibility of peace and justice is kept at bay. 20 There is controversy around the world and, more than ever, I need the solace of your love. 21 I pray that I can use my abilities to further your goodness in the places where I go. 22 But first I must release this discontent and make room for harmony within. 23 Only then will I manifest a positive consciousness.

Anger is a capricious emotion. Sometimes it rises in me and I am unaware of its true source. I am capable of placing anger where it absolutely does not belong. In my self-centeredness I have given it over to another person without owning it or explaining it. This invariably leads to misunderstandings and hurt feelings. In retrospect I remember how much harder it is to correct a wrong than not to do it in the first place. But, I have a little storehouse of unmitigated rage in me, a rage that can come roaring out when I have misplaced my filter. This is mine alone to grapple with, yet I place it on the backs of others, where it never belongs. While I am thankful that this doesn't happen very often, when it does, I live with the corrosive nature of what I have done.

Myrtle Fillmore says this about anger: "One can love and yet become angry. Anger has been misunderstood, and, being out of harmony with life, it becomes destructive. When once the emotion behind the anger is understood, it can be transformed and made an ally of good."[38]

In *The Revealing Word*, Charles Fillmore addresses wrath: "We know that after the destruction of limited and inferior thoughts and forms of life, other and higher thoughts and forms take their place, and the change is actually a blessing in the end. So even the 'wrath' that comes to our fleshly tabernacles, when we persist in holding them in material thought, is ultimately a blessing."[39]

PSALM 75

For the director of music. To the tune of "Do Not Destroy." A psalm of Asaph. A song.

1 Praise and thanksgiving come to you from joyful hearts; your love is the reason for such exclamations. 2 You who are beyond space and time are the giver of life. 3 When I am troubled, I come to you in the silence. You are my foundation. 4 When my personal will is my worst adversary I must pray with a spirit of humility. 5 If I become defiant and stubborn I must pray with a spirit of meekness. 6 When I go forth in a wrong direction and wander in a barren place I must pray with a spirit of willingness. 7 You, God, are my guide and my shepherd. 8 Your love brings vitality to my body and my soul. It is enough to energize me for all my days. 9 Through you,

---

38   Fillmore, Myrtle, *How To Let God Help You*, 62–63.

39   Fillmore, Charles, *The Revealing Word*, 214-215.

The I AM, I am inspired. 10 I will affirm your power and the power of Spirit.

When I read Psalm 75 I think about God's love. Not just that it is always available, but that it is the glue that keeps the cosmos intact and spinning.

These are the words that Charles Fillmore used to define Love:

"Love is a divine attribute; it is an idea in the one Mind. God is love and love is God, or a quality in Being. The difference between divine love and human love is that divine love is broad and unlimited, a universal and harmonizing power...The development of divine love has its place in demonstrating supply. When love is established in the consciousness it will draw to us all that we require to make us happy and contented, all that really belongs to us."[40]

PSALM 76

For the director of music. With stringed instruments. A psalm of Asaph. A song.

1 God is to be praised; God is the source of spiritual truth. 2 With God comes wholeness and perfection, and God gives rise to holy thoughts. 3 God is a wellspring of peace, even in the midst of conflict. 4 From God comes great wisdom and spiritual richness. 5 Prayer and meditation dispel troubles; through them peace is achieved. 6 Disturbance of mind can be settled while praying. 7 With God, fear is denied and the comfort of Spirit is affirmed. 8 Harmony and spiritual discernment are

---

40   Fillmore, Charles, *The Metaphysical Bible Dictionary*, 406.

found while meditating on God's love – 9 God's truth leads to spiritual understanding. 10 Blessings arrive, even in the presence of discord. 11 Affirm God's love and use it to accomplish good works; use your gifts for the betterment of all. 12 Above all, approach God with reverence and awe.

Psalm 76 reflects the wonders of God's awesome strength and infinite capacity. God's creation is governed by laws that keep planets orbiting around suns, and cause stars to be born. That kind of power inspires awe. What is just as inspiring to me is the belief that God also lives within me. Given that, who am I to doubt that I am capable of far more than I believe I am?

With this in mind, I reflect on Unity teachings about affirmations and denials. These are powerful tools for me to use in crafting the direction of my life. Using the strength of God within, I can address both the negative and the positive aspects of my daily life by denying the effects of negative thinking and affirming the gifts that are mine through God's abundance.

Charles Fillmore writes: "A denial is a relinquishment, and it should not be made with too much vehemence. Let us make our denials as though we were gently sweeping away cobwebs, and our affirmations in a strong, bold, positive attitude of mind. When we poise ourselves in Divine Mind, our affirmations and denials will be made in right relation. We will know just when to let go of a thought and when to lay hold of another."[41]

---

41   Fillmore, Charles, *The Revealing Word*, 53.

PSALM 77

For the director of music. For Jeduthun. Of Asaph. A psalm.

1 When I was disturbed I sent my prayers to you, O God. 2 At night I shook with fear and I found no comfort anywhere. 3 I repeated my prayer without stopping, but my fear was increased. 4 I could not close my eyes and sleep; there was no one to whom I could turn. 5 I remembered when my spirit was strong and I was content. 6 But the dark of night covered my soul with unease. I sought God. I asked: 7 "When will this terror end? When will my mind be at ease? 8 Have I forgotten about God's abiding love? Am I cut off from it?" 9 I longed for God's mercy and compassion to comfort me and ease my mind. 10 My distress was not relieved until I went deep into a study of God's truth. 11 I remembered the healing power of faith and I looked for the cause of my distress.12 I went into the silence to find understanding; I approached God with reverence. 13 I restored my belief that communion with God could make me whole again. 14 My thoughts turned away from fear and I affirmed the healing power of Spirit. 15 I opened my mind and soul to the health that lives within me and I released all thoughts of illness. 16 I sought God's living water as a way to cleanse my negative thoughts. 17 Because of this, I felt that I had been washed clean of error thinking. 18 The disturbance that had shaken me so badly receded. 19 I meditated with affirmations of inner harmony and wholeness. 20 With God's help I was drawn from out of affliction and my spiritual strength was restored.

In my middle adult years I was brought down by a severe depression that lasted for months. The worst of my suffering happened in the dark of night, when the children were in bed and the house was quiet. Every night was the same. Anxiety was my companion and sleep was not. I would lie awake for hours, reciting the Lord's Prayer over and over, just to get from one minute to the next. That prayer was the mantle that kept my mind from disintegrating into an overwhelming panic state.

During the day I had a full time job and two children to raise as a single mother, so I could push through the hours, keep my mind occupied, and keep the gloom at bay. But the nights seemed endless and terrifying and stark. Even though I recited the familiar words of the Lord's Prayer, I was not comforted by them. I could not explain to myself why God seemed to have moved so far away as to be unavailable. I felt a profound sense of spiritual loneliness and deprivation.

I went to my minister with questions about how God could have vanished from my awareness. That was my first lesson in understanding that God never leaves me. I took very little consolation from that thought in the beginning, but Bill had planted a seed in my soul. Slowly, over time, that seed took root and grew into a new faith that God is as close as my next breath, that God is found in the silence, and that the darkness is to be respected, but not feared.

PSALM 78

A maskil of Asaph.

1 There is an old story; one with the words of God through-out. 2 The story has many meanings which will be manifest by reading it with wisdom– 3 meanings that have come down through the ages, ones that the ancestors spoke of. 4 This will be recounted as history so that all may know of God's powers that were expressed through ancient people. 5 They spoke of the wisdom that came from God so that people would be guided through their days, 6 so that each generation could tell the next. 7 With this teaching, people would turn to God and live according to God's all-providing law. 8 They would continue to study God's laws and grow in faith. 9 But there were some whose will was strong and not aligned with God; 10 they broke their solemn agreement with God and went their own way. 11 Their memories of God's wonders faded, and they denied God's laws. 12 They saw God's wonders and did not understand; it was as if they were in darkness, and separated from their Source. 13 They kept themselves apart from God and denied the dominion of God. 14 On their journey they were led by the clouds in the daytime and at night they followed the fire light, without believing that it came from God. 15 In the driest desert God split the rocks to give them living water; from the sand God made a river rise. 17 But they denied God's work, thinking only negative thoughts as they wandered in the wilderness. 18 Even so, they demanded food when they were hungry. 19 They taunted God, saying, "Set a table before us!" 20 They denied the source of water and doubted that God could provide sustenance. 21 They continued to deny God, thinking negative thoughts about God's abundance, 22 because they believed more in thoughts of lack. 23 Because of God's mercy the heavens opened; 24 grain grew and they could make bread. 25 The people ate all of the food and were satisfied. 26 They were surrounded by gentle winds, by life-giving east winds. 27 From another direction came plentiful flocks of birds to eat.

28 The birds flew into their camps and were easy to catch. 29 They had an abundance of food to feed their bodies, but their souls still hungered. 30 Because they stayed in the midst of negative thoughts, the food could not sustain them. 31 Some among them died, even those who were strong. 32 Still they dwelt in error, giving importance to thoughts of deprivation and denying God's abundance. 33 More people sickened and died and they all grew very afraid. 34 Sometimes they would turn to God for help, 35 remembering what God had done for them in the wilderness. 36 But they would not keep any solemn agreement with God; 37 they hardened their hearts against God and would not demonstrate a change in their consciousness. 38 God's ability to forgive is endless so they were able to live off of the land. 39 Their earthly bodies lived but their spirits were empty. 40 They continued their worship of material things, yet they still lived in a wilderness. 41 They forgot that all things come from God, and instead kept their covenant with earthly temptations. 42 Over time they forgot the stories of their escape from bondage – how they eluded the oppressor, 43 how they left the land of darkness as God led them forward. 44 They forgot the signs that God gave the oppressor – how the rivers turned blood red and the water was undrinkable. 45 How the insects ate their crops. 47 How the skies opened and wind and hail destroyed more vines. 48 How their livestock were killed by acts of nature. 49 The wrath of God allowed the people to escape and make a new life – for them it was a blessing. 50 But tragedies befell Egypt 51 as the physical health of many was drained and some died. 52 God gave the people their freedom, and they followed along like sheep, 53 while the oppressors were overtaken by a flood.

54 God led them to a place of substance and offered them spiritual wholeness. 55 They were led to a fertile land and settled into homes. 56 They forgot about what God had done for them and refused to consider God's truth. 57 It was easier to stay in sense thoughts and ignore matters of spirit. 58 They began to worship idols that they could see with their eyes and feel with their hands. 59 They turned their backs on God in exchange for earthly goods. 60 But they lost any peace of mind, for they had forsaken God. 61 They would not be open to the spark of divinity that lies within. 62 They began to turn against each other. 63 Men and women forgot the sacred bonds between them; 64 Their priests taught the law but were not good in matters of the spirit. 65 Finally, some among them began to pray and meditate and recognize the God within. 66 They led others in this same way of living. 67 Their minds were opened and their consciousness was raised; 68 They began to live by praising God and giving thanks for God's abundance. 69 Divine Love occupied their thoughts and they were led to God; 70 and recognized God as their shepherd. 71 God sent them a strong leader, 72 and they grew accustomed to walking in the ways of love and justice.

Psalm 78 is a history lesson psalm. It is the well-known story of God's great deeds on behalf of a fractious, ungrateful people. Since I can say that I have behaved that way a few times, it is not for me to criticize or judge. But this is a colossal story of misplaced faith and an absence of gratitude, and the consequences that accompany them both.

In 72 verses, Asaph recounts the Exodus story with all of its miraculous signs of God's commitment to a people. One of the lessons of this story, for me, is the ease with which I can take God's gifts for granted. I get wrapped up in my own complacency and entitlement, fully capable of looking for the easer, softer way to reveal itself. This marks a laziness of spirit in me that inevitable leads nowhere.

Unity tells me that when I give birth to an idea I already have what I need breathe life into it. I can love an idea into being through faith, discernment, discipline, creativity, and a measure of flexibility. For the people of Psalm 78 it was not enough that God provided them with water and grain. Rather than take advantage of the bounty and create a home for themselves, they wanted more to be given to them. I can so easily fall into this trap whenever I forget that God's abundance is all around me.

PSALM 79

A psalm of Asaph.

1 God, when I am aware of evil in the world, all of me is affected; I go within to my place of peace but I am distracted. 2 I see images of death and destruction, of others whose lives have been brutally cut short. 3 Blood stains the streets, there is nothing that I can do. 4 Wickedness abounds and conflict rules. Even from a distance I can feel its effects. 5 How can my prayers change anything? How can I do my part to help those in distress? How can I find you in the middle of a war? 6 I go within to find whatever blessing might result from any of this, and I listen carefully for guidance. 7 But, I often feel helpless when I cannot see a way forward, when my understanding is so dim. 8 Hatred and conflict are handed down from generation to generation – there is no desire for peaceful resolution of age old animosity. 9 Some are known to turn to you, God, trying to find a way out of such calamity. 10 Their prayers go out into the ether, and seem to go unanswered. 11 The cries of the afflicted can be heard by all; they look to you for release. 12 There are those who say that you, God, are too distant; they forget to look within for your love. 13 I will pray that your love be the guiding power whenever there is a true desire for forgiveness.

Some of the psalms are difficult reading for me, and Psalm 79 is one that has challenged me each time I encounter it. When I read verses from thousands of years ago and I can tie them directly to conflicts in this day and age, I see the same traits revealed: desire for power and dominion, cruelty to those who are "different," coveting and seizing land and resources that belong to others, widespread examples of genocide. There is no good explanation for the ways in which havoc and destruction prevail in so many parts of the world.

If only we could forgive one another and commit to a peaceful coexistence. I saw a wonderful example of the power of releasing hatred one evening when I watched a documentary titled, "Forgiving Dr. Mengele." It is about a woman who was imprisoned in a concentration camp and managed to survive the holocaust. She and her twin sister were victims of Joseph Mengele as he conducted inhumane experiments on them. Her twin sister subsequently died from the damage to her body that this man had done.

Decades later she has become a spokesperson for the power of forgiveness. She travels, speaking to audiences about the journey that brought her from rage and hatred to the peace that she has arrived at through her act of declaring amnesty toward Mengele. When she is asked how she can forgive the perpetrators of such horrors she simply says, "It has nothing to do with them." She goes on to describe how letting go of her anger has allowed her to reclaim her life. She has consciously changed her reality from living as a victim to a dweller in a place of peace and compassion. She has set out to change her story so she can live, fully alive and unafraid.

PSALM 80

For the director of music. To the tune of "The Lilies of the Covenant." Of Asaph. A psalm.

1 Those who are innocent are cared for by God and are given understanding and vitality. 2 Their faith grows in their consciousness because they are able to balance holy understanding and human will. 3 With prayer and meditation they are in God's presence and feel secure. 4 They commune with God about their human emotions and receive guidance when they are disturbed. 5 When they are weeping and suffering, they turn to God for help. 6 Sometimes others do not understand the depth of their faith; they speak words of criticism about them. 7 The devout ones ask to be transformed by God's light and love. 8 They are like a vine that branches forth and bears fruit. 9 When they receive God's wisdom in their hearts, they are producers of good. 10 This goodness passes from person to person and grows in power and influence. 11 There are no boundaries to where goodwill can go; it benefits any who come in contact with it. 12 It must be tended carefully and used with integrity. 13 Goodness cannot be twisted or misused, it can only be of help when it is offered with love. 14 God supports anyone who relies on Divine Mind for direction. 15 When in the silence, there are those who search for the Christ, the perfect expression of God. 16 Their faith grows stronger as their understanding deepens. 17 They live on the side of truth and look for the Christ in others. 18 They praise your name and honor your abundance. 12 By following your wisdom, people will be sanctified.

When I read Psalm 80, I am reminded of St. Francis of Assisi. He was a man who seemingly had it all: wealth, station in life, and opportunities. Yet, he gave it all up to become the groom whose bride was poverty. He turned to a life of innocence and simplicity.

For days at a time, Francis would retreat to a cave to fast and to commune with God. His companion, Brother Leo, would check on him by listening at the mouth of the cave to make sure that Francis was still alive. He would hear Francis weeping, and telling his fears and his doubts to God.

Francis would cry out to God and say that he was not worthy of the mission given to him. In the solitude, he would voice his doubts, his unfit nature, his wavering convictions. Then he would emerge from the cave refreshed and filled with the energy he needed to live a life of poverty while delighting in the marvels of creation. Francis understood the beauty of simplicity and the importance of a constant search for God's truth.

PSALM 81

For the director of music. According to gittith. Of Asaph.

1 It is time to sing out thanks to God; to set a harmony within while praising God! 2 When music sends its vibrations through us, we are calmed and Spirit comes to us. 3 We open to the power of Spirit within us, our minds ready to receive Spirit's healing balm. 4 It is good for all people to come close to God and raise up spiritual consciousness. 5 Sense thinking is released to make room for God's truth and God's Word, for God speaks to us in many ways. 6 God's presence helps to settle worries and to free the mind from troubled thoughts. 7 The power of God's love erases any doubts that God is within us and around us. 8 When we seek God's truth with open minds, our spiritual consciousness is enhanced. 9 We need not worship false gods; we remain faithful to the one true God. 10 We affirm that with God's abundance we always have just what we need to live a good life. 11 When negative thoughts enter our consciousness, prayer and meditation reduce thoughts of adversity. 12 When we honor the love that comes from the heart we are in Spirit's presence. 13 We enter the silence to hear the word of God and we are satisfied. 14 Acknowledging God's presence and power strengthens our body, mind, and spirit. 15 We are able to deny fear and error, and release that which harms us. 16 Our souls feed on the bread of heaven and confirm the sweetness of God's abiding love.

My favorite way to pray is to sing. I have had opportunities to belong to church choirs for decades, and I am convinced that my life is richer because of this blessing. Learning the music improves my brain's abilities, and learning the words sends prayers into the ether. Putting words and music together enhances creativity. A skilled choir director prepares the offering for both God and congregation. And, the singers can praise God directly from the heart! It doesn't get much better than this.

PSALM 82

A psalm of Asaph.

1 God is present in the sanctuary; when we join God there, we open ourselves to a greater possibility of spiritual growth. 2 We are called by God to avoid injustice and to set aside error thoughts. 3 We are guided to support those who are weak and alone; to share our bounty and to work for justice. 4 We are to give to those in need and raise them up in our prayers and with our actions. 5 While we may be surrounded by false claims, we do not put our belief in them. We search for enlightenment instead. 6 If we give too much power to idols we will cut ourselves off from spiritual development. 7 We will forget to act according to God's law; we will lose sight of the life force within. 8 However, when our spirit is open to them, we receive divine ideas from God and we are able to live according to God's goodness.

Psalm 82 speaks to me about temptation and about making choices based on empty promises. But it reminds me that even when my head is turned toward glitter and glamor, God is with me. This is the sure knowledge that surrounded Jesus while he was in the desert, fasting and praying, and confronted by a force that tried to shake loose his allegiance to God. It was this faith that drove him to deny the powers of those false claims that were laid before him.

I also am reminded again about my little-g gods. Following them is like counting on a dead-end street to get me where I need to go. Instead, when I follow God I am led to focus on the kind of justice that honors creation and supports my fellow travelers.

If we are to live as a people of justice and faith, the call is clear: take care of the least of us and support those in need. In South Africa there is a concept called "Ubuntu," and it goes something like this: I am human because you are who you are as a human being. If you are hungry, I share what I have. We live together as an interdependent community. I benefit from your talents and you benefit from mine. Together, we live out God's covenant.

PSALM 83

A song. A psalm of Asaph.

1 Our cry goes out to you, O God; we seek understanding, we need your wisdom. 2 Those who speak against your ways make their presence known loudly. 3 Their clever words are meant to cast doubt upon you; they conspire to demean you. 4 They say, "God's followers are weak, and they can be swayed, they will forget their God." 5 They gather to plan their rallies, to form alliances with others who think as they do. 6 Some are tied to sense consciousness and place great value on material things. 7 Some have beliefs that lead to lawless behaviors and selfish gain. 8 Their thoughts are undisciplined and not illumined by Spirit. 9 Some aggressively seek to dominate others; their thoughts are fixed and not easily changed. 10 They do not want to consider a realm of the spirit. 11 They are driven by greed and tainted by error. 12 They scheme and plot to destroy any evidence of your powers of creation. 13 Their plans change like the wind, but they are steeped in evil. 14 God, send the fire of Spirit to cleanse and purify them, 15 so that your love will enter their hearts, and they may be free from fear. 16 Cover them with your goodness; let their plotting become prayers. 17 Soften their thoughts so that they may accept your abundance.

18 Help them to change their allegiance to false idols so that they may experience the power of your truth.

The world is occupied by so many factions, all seeking to destroy an enemy. There are wars over the right to occupy each other's territory. Fences are erected, sabers are rattled, bombs are deployed, people displaced, genocides initiated, embargos imposed, peace talks held and then cancelled. Years go by and no acceptable resolution can be found. The leaders of the nations seem powerless to effect any change.

Things are not that different now than in ancient times. In the NIV version of this psalm there are at least 17 names of warriors and battles fought over a piece of real estate and the right to claim victory. Each of these names and places can be found in Charles Fillmore's *Metaphysical Bible Dictionary*. It is not a coincidence that the metaphysical definition of all of them had to do with consciousness of the senses, and a corresponding lack of any spiritual influence. As I re-visioned Psalm 83, the themes of error thinking and selfishness emerged repeatedly.

PSALM 84

For the director of music. According to gittith. Of the Sons of Korah. A psalm.

1 God dwells in us all, a holy spark of goodness lies within. 2 With my eyes I see beauty around me and with my inner eye I see truth; my spirit is strengthened when I behold God's Creation. 3 Every creature is precious in God's sight; even the tiniest bird will find a home and build a nest. 4 Those who honor and care for creation will find a sacred space in which to live. 5 Blessings come to those who earnestly seek God, who cannot be distracted from this quest. 6 Even if they walk with troubled hearts they search for God's streams of living water, and when they find them their hearts are refreshed. 7 They pray to God and their whole being is strengthened. 8 I lift my prayers to you, O God; I pray for greater understanding of your ways. 9 Everywhere I look I see signs of your Divine Law. 10 I am blessed by your presence; I would rather meditate on your Word than follow false claims. 11 With you, God, my mind and spirit are illumined; I learn the best use of my abilities and I work for good. 12 My trust in you is my blessing.

When I read Psalm 84 I am always lifted up. I am reminded that no matter where I am, I am at home with God. To me, home is any place where God's presence can be felt, or seen, or heard. And, Psalm 84 reminds me that a "place" is not as important as my state of mind when I am there.

Where my heart and soul find gladness is inevitably in moments of kindness, in the singing of God's songs, in the presence of compassion, in the early morning silence, in the pages of a book that prods my thinking, in between the beats of my music, and, especially, in the presence of God's love.

My goal is to go from day to day with a resilient heart, a heart that can experience both joy and sorrow and all the in-betweens. I know that in order to do this, I must rely on a wisdom greater than mine. There are many ways to find this wisdom and I have used them. Whether it's as simple as taking a deep breath or as challenging as mending some fence I have trampled over, it is all worth the effort. For those moments when nothing seems to work to ease my troubled mind, I remember "this too shall pass."

PSALM 85

For the director of music. Of the Sons of Korah. A psalm.

1 God, I look around and see your handiwork everywhere; you are the source of all life. 2 From your love comes forgiveness, and with prayer comes understanding of error. 3 Your presence can dispel my fears and soothe my temper. 4 When I commune with you my troubles are eased. 5 If I ask for discernment when I am angry, will I be open to it? If I persist in my discontent, will I find release? 6 When I am troubled, if I truly believe in your love will my wayward faith be restored? 7 I do not doubt your goodness and my hope for redemption persists. 8 I go into the silence to receive your Word; I am open to your wisdom – I will renounce my foolish thoughts. 9 I will affirm my abilities and I will rely on Spirit's guidance. 10 Through your love, my faith is strengthened beyond imagination; I want only to walk on a path of harmony. 11 I know that you are present on earth and throughout the cosmos. 12 And, in your presence there is only abundance. 13 I will turn my consciousness to your truth, and in so doing I will step forth with confidence.

I find a theme of forgiveness in Psalm 85. There are many words that mean forgiveness: amnesty, charity, compassion, exoneration, grace, mercy, reprieve, respite, pardon, absolution, clemency, atonement. These are just a few words that help to explain the love of God demonstrated in daily life. As I am a part of God's creation, then, the manifestation of forgiveness lives within me. I have access to the grace of seeing beyond my own hurt, or my sense of being wronged; knowing this to be true makes me better able to understand the context in which I feel slighted. I am more likely to search within for my own part in the drama.

One of the benefits of forgiveness is an inner peace at having set rancor aside in exchange for pardon. Sometimes this peace is not all that easy to attain. First I must be willing to examine the hurt and anger that I feel. More importantly, I must be willing to consider my own actions toward the other person, and accept that I may have contributed to the disagreement. The depth of my wounded-ness will dictate the amount of inner work that faces me as I strive for that precious resolution. There is no better place to start than with prayer and meditation.

PSALM 86

A prayer of David.

1 I come to you, God, when I am unsure of myself and in need of your guidance. 2 In the silence I affirm your healing power; 3 with that comes mercy and the assurance of your presence. 4 I rely on your presence and it brings me joy. 5 There is a never-ending source of love and goodness emanating from you. 6 My prayer to you is one of deep gratitude for the wisdom that comes while in the silence. 7 When I am troubled, I meditate on your love. 8 I bring my flaws into your light and pray that they may be corrected. 9 When my thoughts are tied in knots I come to you for guidance; you are the source of true wisdom. 10 I marvel at the clarity that comes when I meditate with you. 11 Truth comes to me and my heart and soul are lifted in divine unity. 12 When I speak of you I use words of praise and thanksgiving. 13 Your love brings me out from my darkest places and I am at peace. 14 For those times when I have erred, I know that I can ask for forgiveness; I can learn to step away from error. 15 There is no end to your compassion and love. 16 I live in your presence and I am secure; I pray that my actions are comforting to others. 17 All around me there is evidence of your love for creation; there is nothing for me to fear for you are merciful.

Calling out to God from a place of discomfort and distress means I must acknowledge that the only thing I control is my willingness to ask for help. That, in turn, requires me to understand and believe that by humbling myself I become stronger.

When I am filled with arrogance, I have plowed through my days and missed out on the richness that comes when I am wise enough to seek counsel.

For me, Psalm 86 is also a perspective psalm. It is about seeing the evidence of God's love and abundance. It is about learning to value what I have and what I need to give away in service of God's truth.

I have learned that for every ache I experience, there are people whose pain is far worse. For every benefit I have been given there is someone who needs it more urgently. For everything I think I must have, there is a far better use for my money. For all of my opinions and judgments there are kinder ways to structure my thoughts and my actions. I believe that these are the lessons that appear to me with regularity. It is only when I pay attention to what God's truth tells me that I am a true contributor to the forward motion of creation.

PSALM 87

Of the Sons of Korah. A psalm. A song.

1 God provides spiritual realization to those who seek it. 2 God is found where love abides, where holy thoughts and ideals dwell. 3 There, God's Word is revealed when the soul is ready to receive it. 4 When material consciousness prevails, the realm of imagination is not illumined; Spirit comes, but is turned away. Not until truth is sought will there be spiritual understanding. 5 When higher consciousness is developed, God's abundant wisdom is made known. 6 The ones who search for God will know the presence of Spirit. 7 They will sing songs of praise and exaltation.

Psalm 87 has always resonated with me as being a song about finding one's place in God's creation. Unity teaches me that we are all children of God, with no exceptions and no exclusions. This leads me to believe that my place in God's cosmos is right where I am at the moment. Wherever I am, I am in my spiritual home.

I grew up overseas, in Mexico and Brazil. It was a life of many transitions, where people came and went with regularity. Before I was 16 I had emigrated to three countries. What I learned from those experiences was to burrow in wherever I am and try to make a home where I find myself planted.

It occurs to me that we are all immigrants from the time we are born. We come into an unfamiliar place, we have to learn at least one language, we learn about the customs of our particular home and environment, and sometimes we have to make our way without a map or a guide.

When I retired from nursing I found a new career that called to me loudly and insistently. These days I volunteer for an immigration attorney. Our main job is to help people find their way through the convoluted immigration laws of the United States of America. Doing this work I have heard stories of amazing courage from people who left home and family with the hope of making a better life here and improving the lives of those left behind.

Some people are escaping circumstances that are life threatening and are praying that they won't be sent back to face certain harm, or even death. As they journey toward us they encounter many dangers on the way: robbery, beatings, rapes, and physical injuries, to name a few. Many of them cross our border into the most inhospitable desert landscapes and thousands have lost their lives in the process. Those who do find a place somewhere in our society live in constant fear of being discovered and sent away.

I believe we are doing God's work in our little law office. We do what we can to help people stay here, where they have made homes and are raising families. We try to make it possible for them to bloom where they are planted. I believe this is what God asks of us all, to be hospitable, to be loving, and to accept the richness of blending cultures. After all, God's love knows no borders.

PSALM 88

A song. A psalm of the Sons of Korah. For the director of music. According to mahalath leannoth. A maskil of Heman the Ezrahite.[42]

1 God, my life is at its lowest ebb and I pray to you for relief. 2 My prayers are for you alone, God, for you alone can rescue me. 3 My mind is filled with thoughts of my last breath and I am afraid. 4 Others think of me as dead already, my weakness is so profound. 5 My mind dwells in sorrow and I feel far away from your presence. 6 I fear that I am in a deep and dark pit from which I cannot rise. 7 I know that I must pray about your mercy before I am completely engulfed by my sorrow. 8 When I find no one to help me I must enter the silence with faith in your healing ways. 9 I must find my way back to a place where I can acknowledge my power again. 10 I must meditate on your Law and free myself from error thoughts. 11 I must affirm your love, knowing that it is the true breath of life. 12 The light of your wisdom will shine for me again, and when I am restored I will praise you. 13 I will pray that the energy of life is within me, and I will meditate on restoring health to my body. 14 When I think that I cannot find you, I must remember that you are as close as my very breath. 15 I have been a slave to false thoughts; I must think only thoughts of healing and redemption. 16 I will deny that fear accompanies me; instead, I will affirm your divine guidance. 17 I will spend my day meditating in the precious silence; I will not be

---

42 Heman: "Thoughts full of faith and trust in God, thoughts that are honest, true, steadfast, accurate. Great wisdom and harmony are the result of these thoughts." *Metaphysical Bible Dictionary*, 272.

overcome by thoughts of disease and illness. 18 My compan-
ions will be your angels, and I will know your truth.

There is no mention in Psalm 88 about what may have engulfed the writer in such sorrow. There is no way of identifying what brought the writer down so far into such despair. Unity teaches me that my very thoughts and my state of mind are determining factors in how I feel, just as important as the condition of illness itself. I am reminded of the power of imaging positive circumstances and denying thoughts of lack and illness. However, I can't in all honesty say that I remember to do this all the time. Sometimes I just need to reflect on my demons and give them a name. I believe this weakens them and strengthens me. Having done that, I am better prepared to make a plan that seeks God's guidance. Then it is much easier for me to pray specifically for what I need to overcome whatever is troubling me.

During my days as a hospice nurse I often sat with patients and family members who were trying to reason out why such suffering had been meted out to them, or to someone they loved. Thoughts of a last breath sometimes led to a request to put an end to endless suffering, to speed the process along, to reach the ultimate relief. In the face of such distress I struggled with the shadow side of my code of ethics, but my responsibility lay with creating comfort measures designed to alleviate suffering as much as humanly possible.

I once cared for a woman who had been my nursing director for 13 years. We met again under very different circumstances. Her body was being ravaged by a vicious autoimmune disease and hospice was her last remaining hope for any quality of life to be had. One day we were sitting quietly together because it was hard for her to talk and because I had nothing helpful to say. So we sat in a fellow nursey silence, both of us wise to what was coming. Suddenly, she stirred a little and asked me this question: "Did I do a good job?" I knew what she was asking. In the last days of her life she was considering what her contribution had been to the profession that she cherished, and the people that she led. She needed to know that her life had meant something, that she had somehow made a difference. I will always hope that my answer was the comfort that she needed.

PSALM 89

A maskil of Ethan the Ezrahite.[43]

1 God is the source of love; God's faithfulness never falters. 2 God's love extends to all creation, God brings harmony to all who seek it. 3 Those who are filled with divine love honor a covenant with God, 4 their spiritual body will endure forever. 5 Their thoughts will be of spiritual matters and they will be sought for their wisdom. 6 Their gift will be to speak the word of God to all who will listen. 7 They will demonstrate the glory of God through their actions and words. 8 Their counsel will be of value to many because of their faithfulness. 9 They have moved beyond thoughts of physical being and live within the domain of Spirit. 10 They are not caught in the realm of error for they have elevated their consciousness. 11 They declare that heaven is within each person, open to all who are attracted to matters of spirit. 12 Wherever they are they live to revere Divine Mind, the source of All That Is. 13 They are powerful

---

43 Ethan the Ezrahite: "Ethan the Ezrahite was a wise man in Solomon's time (IKings 4:31)...Intellectual understanding, which is natural to man in his seemingly mortal state (a native, i.e., in his own country). One may become very brilliant in so far as education and the intellect are concerned, yet fall far short of the true spiritual wisdom that Solomon signifies." *Metaphysical Bible Dictionary*, 214.

because they are on the side of truth. 14 They work for justice, and righteousness is their foundation. 15 They have learned the power of communion with God, and they are blessed. 16 They bring forth God's name when it is needed. 17 Their souls rest in God's goodness and they give thanks always. 18 God is the protector of all creation, giving life to those who believe. 19 Strength also comes from God, when there is harmony between body and spirit. 20 God's love settles a troubled soul whenever there is communion with God. 21 God's sustaining presence surrounds each one and from it comes comfort and security. 22 Therefore the faithful will not be swayed by false claims. 23 They will affirm God's truth and they will draw close to divine ideas. 24 God's love is omnipresent, and is the foundation of creation. 25 When thoughts are of a purely spiritual nature, they lead to the river of life. 26 The ones who know this to be true will be renewed. 27 Their lives will be guided by Spirit. 28 Their bond with God will be strengthened. 29 Their children will be blessed. 30 Those who use error as a guide do not follow God's truth, 31 and do not honor Spirit. 32 They may live with thoughts of lack; their path may lead them to sin.33 Even so, God's love is never far from them - they have ability to live in it. 34 All who enter into the silence with God will find redemption when they meditate on divine law. 35 God's truth is to be sought through prayer and communion with Spirit. 36 This truth is eternal and infinite. 37 It is as reliable as the moon's path through the night sky. 38 Those who are contrary to God's law of Being do not live within higher thinking. 39 They do not desire a covenant of any kind, except for their allegiance to material gain. 40 They are on a path of destruction. 41 They are not good neighbors. 42 They are not peacemakers. 43 They live with anger in their very being. 44 They are not caretakers of creatures or belongings. 45 They are not stewards of their health or wellbeing. 46 They question the very existence of God and demand proof of God's powers. 47 They live in fear of their own ending and find little meaning in their lives. 48 They are drawn to thoughts of illness and unrest. 49 They do not think about God's love, nor do they look for God's blessings. 50 Not so those who walk in God's ways; they will feel God's love around them. 51 They will keep their thoughts aligned with truth and they will work for good. 52 They will praise God's name forever. Amen

Psalm 89 is an enigma to me. For 37 verses, I read a description of people of great faith, and of the practices that make them devout. Then, in verse 38 the focus changes. Suddenly, the psalm is describing people who choose to live a life apart from God. Their flaws are laid out in great detail. This detour is hard to align with the rest of the psalm. Sometimes I wonder if two psalms were somehow melded into one.

The basis of many psalms is the covenant that exists between the people of Israel and God. When I consider Psalm 89 in this light I am reminded that I, too, live in relationship with my Creator. With the blessings of prayer and meditation and the insights that come to me, I am given the opportunity to live my best life. But I stumble and get distracted and my sense of entitlement governs my behavior. Before long I am trying to paint God into a corner, having overstepped the bounds of arrogance. My flaws bloom forth and I am temporarily lost.

The God of my being and of my limited understanding never leaves me there for long. Intuitively I know that I have stepped off my usual path.

How this message is delivered depends on the degree to which I have stopped listening to that still, small voice. I know this to be true because sometimes its arrival is as subtle as a butterfly's landing, and sometimes it is by way of the jolt of a rough lesson.

Chapter Five

BOOK IV
Psalms 90–106

PSALM 90

A prayer of Moses the man of God.[44]

1 From our beginning we are each an expression of Divine Mind. 2 We come from Divine Substance that manifested as the earth that we know – the mountains, the seas, and the creatures that inhabit them. 3 When we are finished with our bodies, they return to the dust from whence they came. 4 Time is but a pattern put upon infinity, but God is eternal. 5 When our bodies are empty and still, we have gone on to newness. 6 We are born in the morning, and gone with the darkest night. 7 God's fire burns through us and we are purified.

---

44 Moses: "Moses means drawing out, extracting, i.e., from the water. The birth of Moses represents man's development in consciousness of the law of his being, from the negative side. Water represents universal negation; but water also represents the great possibility. Out of seemingly negative conditions comes the new growth." *Metaphysical Bible Dictionary*, 460-461.

8 We commune with God to manifest thoughts of goodness and abundance; we transform our error thoughts. 9 We are given a new day in which to call forth Spirit, and lift our consciousness. 10 We do not know the number of our days; but each one is an opportunity to choose between darkness and light. 11 God's wrath exists only as a purifying force, consuming that which does not serve us, and leaving us with higher thoughts to consider. 12 If we knew how long we would be on this earthly plane we would begin the search for God's wisdom early in our years. 13 We are not to know this, only that each day can be used for good, and that we can be compassionate beings. 14 God's love never falters. From this we will get joy, and be grateful for each day.15 Whenever we are troubled, we have only to go within to that still place where we will find both God and Spirit. 16 We are also to look outside of ourselves at all the expressions of God's abundance. 17 Learning from God, we will find our purpose and the work that we do will be of service – yes, our work will be blessed.

Psalm 90 is the only one attributed to Moses, without whom history would read differently. For Moses, life was a series of challenges that he faced with courage and conviction. His belief in a Creator God must have sustained him through slavery and exodus and the call to lead a tribe of nomads into an unfamiliar wilderness. Seas parting, burning bushes, holy ground, stone tablets, manna from heaven are just a few of the highlights of his life. This man knew the meaning of trust and hard work and persistence!

I think of Psalm 90 as the "dust to dust" prayer, a reminder of just how fleeting this lifetime is in the grand scheme of things. A most powerful image of this reality came to me some 50 years ago when, as a teenager,

I stood on the rim of the Grand Canyon and looked down into its depths. Our guide was telling us that when we reached the bottom, we would have passed through eons of layers of time. And, when we got to the bottom, we could touch the basalt rock that is a billion + years old. That was a visual and spiritual perspective that has stayed with me for all these years.

These days I have more years behind me than I have years ahead of me. Sometimes I think about when breath leaves my body for the last time. The atoms that were once me will scatter; a spark of my energy lives on in my children, and the rest of it will rejoin the infinite energy that is God.

PSALM 91

1 There is a place of rest and safety that is found when entering the silence with God. 2 It is there for me when I quiet myself and wait to feel God's presence. 3 I have nothing to fear – troubles of mind and body fade when I pray. 4 When I meditate, I am comforted; I know that with God I am protected. 5 Night and day God is with me and my worries will diminish when I affirm God's energy within me; 6 healing happens when I believe in God's restorative powers. 7 Even if illness is all around me, the words of my prayers protect me from harm. 8 I turn away from error thoughts and my affirmations bring me strength. 9 I believe that God is the source of all good, 10 and through discernment I am made aware of this. 11 When I am open to God's truth I raise my consciousness to a higher level. 12 Even when I am in pain, there is opportunity for healing. 13 I do not give strength to my worries; I find courage through prayer and meditation. 14 God's love surrounds me and lives within me; I affirm this truth. 15 My

prayers are answered, sometimes in unexpected ways, if I am
open to God's endless possibilities. 16 All my days are ordered
when I gratefully receive God's gifts.

Psalm 91 brings a powerful declaration of God's grace, that mantle of love and compassion that is always there, both seen and intuited. I know that I have been the beneficiary of this gift. I can recall so many occasions when my fear or unrest have been calmed by an unspoken affirmation, or by a sense that "this too shall pass," or by a deep knowing that whatever the outcome, it will be born through grace. I can go through my life with the faith that I will have what I need, be it strength, or courage, or the peace that comes with acceptance.

My sense is that there have been so many unseen blessings, those times when I am unaware of having been lifted up. Without knowing it, I have been carried to safety. Maybe I know this from a place with no words, from a belief on a cellular level that the laws of God's creation run through me like a river on its way to the sea

PSALM 92

A psalm. A song. For the Sabbath day.[45]

1 Songs of praise to God bring happiness to those who sing
and those who listen. 2 Words of thanks, set to music, are
holy prayers, 3 and stringed instruments are the wings that

---

45 Sabbath: "The Sabbath is a very certain definite thing. It is a state of mind that man enters or acquires when he goes into the silence of his own soul, into the realm of Spirit. There he finds true rest and peace. The seventh day means the seventh or perfect stage of one's spiritual unfoldment." *Metaphysical Bible Dictionary*, 563.

carry them forth. 4 In the midst of God's abundance there is joy, while creation manifests the love that God sends out to all. 5 Divine Mind is the source of All That Is, and it is absolute. 6 There are those to whom the laws of creation are foreign, whose understanding is limited to sense consciousness. 7 To them, false claims ring true and they follow them to their end. 8 Surely with God our thoughts are elevated to higher planes, 9 but those who doubt the love and goodness of God will not know peace. 10 I have been lifted up when I affirm the power of Spirit. 11 My senses are open to receive God's abundance and I am at peace. 12 The Spirit of God brings health to my body and soul; 13 my trust in God strengthens my entire being. 14 I will pray for the honor of working for good in God's world, 15 knowing neither fear nor doubt, and I will sing praises until my voice is no more.

Psalm 92 is written for the Sabbath day, a concept that has fallen by the wayside in our 24/7/365 world. We choose our days of rest and contemplation in between our life's demands. For some, there is no day of rest, there is just another day spent figuring out how to survive the next 24 hours. Only the most devout/orthodox people make the Sabbath hours a devotional to God, a day in which to reflect the best ways in which to honor God.

A friend once told me that she needed to go on a retreat, before she "lost her center." The word "retreat" can symbolize a time away from the cumulative exhaustions of everyday life. For my friend, she needed a bit of time to rearrange the puzzle pieces so that the picture of her life would emerge as she imagined it to be. For her, she needed to gather in her threads and do some re-weaving before the bare spots were beyond repair. Surely that day of rest and contemplation can become a sacred ritual!

PSALM 93

1 Divine Mind is omnipresence; from it comes all that is, seen and unseen, known and unknown; the earth and the heavens are manifestations of it. 2 With God, there is no time; there is no measure of eternity. 3 God is the source of the divine energy that creates the cosmos; God's wisdom keeps the stars in their courses; God's truth is the source of all knowledge. 4 There is no strength like the strength that comes from God – with it, there are endless possibilities. 5 The Word of God expresses perfection; with it comes wholeness of body, mind, and spirit.

Psalm 93 leaves no doubt as to who is in charge of infinity and eternity. With our magnificent brains we try to understand that there is no beginning and no end, but we are transient beings and we need some way to measure our individual lifetimes. I want to understand things from a beginning, middle, and ending perspective. Only when my mind wanders into sacred space can I intuit infinity as Truth.

Some years ago I took my children to Ireland. Being a Murphy by birth I thought it was time for us to explore one of our countries of origin. One day we decided to go off the beaten track and go exploring. As we were driving we saw a small sign pointing toward a hill. The sign invited us to turn on to a dirt road that would lead us to "passage tombs."

Somehow we had come across an ancient burial site. After a rigorous climb we found ourselves on top of a hill, with an expansive view of the countryside below. The ground was covered with heather, and there were mounds of rocks that were clearly man made. We had discovered Carrowkeel, in County Sligo. We learned later that it is a site that has been confirmed to be 5,100 to 5,400 years old. This pre-dates the pyramids in Egypt by several hundred years.

We were the only people there. No caretaker, no fences, no restrictions, no guided tour. My children were able to crawl into one of the tombs. They knew to be respectful and not take anything they might find in the rocky passage or in the chamber. The only thing they took was a picture that showed the light pouring in from the entryway. Meanwhile, I wandered around the hilltop transfigured by the beauty and the holiness of this remote place. I felt with absolute certainty that I had been here before. I felt a kinship with the makers of the rustic tombs. Mostly, though, I felt a great love and respect for the people that had come before, and had chosen such a sacred place in which to rest.

PSALM 94

1 God is not a God of vengeance, but a God of mercy and compassion. 2 But those who live with arrogance will find it hard to understand God's truth. 3 Those who live without kindness will not know true joy. 4 They use harsh words and treat others with disdain. 5 Although they are surrounded by God's love, they are unaware of its presence. 6 They turn their backs on those from whom there is nothing to gain. 7 They do not seek God in the silence, and they close themselves off from Spirit. 8 They follow false claims, searching only for material gain. 9 They answer to no one, believing that they are the source of consciousness. 10 Do they not see that God is good? Do they not feel the spark of their own divinity? 11 God is omnipresence; all of creation manifests from God's substance. 12 Blessings come when God's presence is recognized and God's wisdom is sought. 13 Prayers and affirmations lead to greater spiritual understanding. 14 God's love is there for anyone who opens heart and soul to receive it. 15 With meditation comes spiritual discernment, and the seeker will welcome it. 16 Who will stand up for kindness? Who will work for justice? 17 Without knowledge of God I would live only in sense consciousness. 18 Without prayer I would have nowhere to turn for counsel. 19 When I am deeply troubled, I find release from those bonds as I meditate on them. 20 God's wisdom is omniscient – if I seek it, how can I fail? 21 If I am in the presence of evil, I turn to Spirit for guidance. 22 As I enter the silence I can release thoughts that no longer serve me, and I find rest. 23 In God's presence, I learn to let go of error thoughts; I can affirm God's truth and be uplifted.

From thousands of years ago, the poet asks who will be kind, and who will work for justice? For the writers of the Psalms, oppression and injustice were part of the fabric of their lives and their history. Impassioned pleas for help from God were sometimes the only recourse left. Running through this psalm is the belief that God's foundation is firm, even in the face of evil. Surrounded by wickedness, the poet knows that turning to God is a haven in itself.

PSALM 95

1 When we gather together in God's name it is a joyous occasion. 2 By praising God through word or song we show our

gratitude; we are given what we need to be freed from limita-
tions. 3 Divine Mind is the architect of the universe, the creator
of All That Is. 4 From the valleys to the highest peaks we see
evidence of God's great work. 5 The sea and its mysteries are
God's manifestation as well. 6 We bring our prayers to God
and we approach God with humility. 7 Because of God's abun-
dance we are given what we need. 8 When we turn away from
God, temptation and doubt can enter our being, 9 and we rely
on error thinking. 10 When such thoughts are lasting, we do
not approach God and Spirit for our guidance. 11 We forget
that God's truth is the only eternal Absolute.

Psalm 95 is a psalm of invitation to marvel at God's creative powers and
to worship God in community. It is a time to join together in proclaiming
the power of God's love and the hope for redemption. That we are created
by God, and that redemption is available to all are two critical tenets of
my faith.

I have an easier time with the first one, as God's creation is evident everywhere that I look. I can't turn my back on it and pretend I don't belong.
Redemption is sometimes a concept that I don't completely grasp: is it a
state of being? Can true redemption only come from God? When is the
right time to ask for it? Once granted, is it forever?

Psalm 95 takes a turn away from praising God and moves into a caution-
ary mode. I am reminded there are consequences that come when I take
God for granted and when I expect more for less effort on my part. This is
where the covenant piece of my faith comes to the forefront. I live in relationship with God; I am given what I need to live a clean life; I am given
the power of choice. It's on me.

I can always choose between God and my various little-g gods. I know very well what the wiser course is. The evidence is everywhere around me that when I devote heart and mind to seeking God's way, my efforts bear a sweeter fruit. My mind is more peaceful and focused, my heart fuller and more content. After the fact, I am always astounded and chagrined when I have given in to my lesser self.

PSALM 96

1 All voices of Creation rise up in song and sing praise to God, the I AM. 2 Setting words of adoration to music brings the glory of God to all who listen. 3 It is good to proclaim the unity of people with God, who manifests abundance. 4 God is absolute Divine Mind; there is no other God. 5 We know about false gods who are contrary to God's truth, for God is the creator of All That Is. 6 Through God we are given freedom from illusion; we see with clear eyes the magnificence of God. 7 No one is excluded from the kingdom; all that is needed is faith. 8 As consciousness is refined we give thanks; in God's house our thoughts are purified. 9 Our spirits are made whole; we are humbled in the presence of God's goodness. 10 We speak of God's love for all. The earth and all that dwell on it are blessed by love's omnipresence. 11 The universe vibrates with God's manifestations; the stars, the planets, the seas and the mountains are all created from holy substance. 12 Joy prevails throughout as seeds become the food from the fields; even the trees dance when God's purifying wind moves their branches. 13 It is good to rejoice and praise God, the God that lives within. When we come to God in prayer, when we come

to God in meditation, we find a state of harmony and our
faith flourishes.

When I attend Unity services I come away uplifted, having been reminded in some way that God is the radiant energy of creation. Psalm 96 tells a similar story about God's unending love that is in constant motion, creating and re-creating in an infinite pattern, at work in the vastness of the universe.

In the *Metaphysical Bible Dictionary*, Charles Fillmore says this about Creation:

"Creation presupposes a creator. The creator is God, Divine Mind. God creates by the power of his word: 'God said...and it was so.'...The character of God's creation is 'good' and 'very good'. There is no other creator than God. He made all that is. God's creation was in the realm of ideas, in the ideal, in mind."[46]

Unity teaches me that I, too, am a creator. Ideas or images come to me and I always have the opportunity to turn a thought into a reality. Several years into my hospice nursing experience, I noticed a certain fatigue of spirit. I loved my work deeply, but the cumulative effect of the sorrows that attend this type of vocation had gradually worn me down. I felt a somberness in my soul that was out of character for me.

The idea came to me that I needed something colorful and joyful to do, as a hobby. One day I was on Main Street in St. Charles, Missouri, and I walked past a stained glass supply store. In the window was a sign about lessons

---

46   *Metaphysical Bible Dictionary*, 158.

in creating stained glass pieces. Before I knew it, I was in the store, signing up for a class.

What followed was a period of several years when I made many pieces. The process of choosing a pattern, finding the colors of glass to start with, and cutting each piece to fit gave me such pleasure. There were evenings when hours would go by unnoticed as I carefully turned sheets of beautiful glass into a manifestation of a finished product. As I worked, I felt a connection with God's creative energy as it flowed through me into a carefully cut bit of color and light.

This experience was a reminder that we each have the power to create something into existence. This is one of God's gifts, freely given to us as the same love that manifests the stars.

PSALM 97

1 God is with me in body, mind and soul; there is no distance between us. 2 When I am in great turmoil I turn to God; God's infinite love is my foundation. 3 If my thoughts turn to materiality, God's purifying fire consumes my false assumptions. 4 I see that the power of God's spiritual and natural laws is evident throughout creation. 5 Even in my distress, when I pray I increase my awareness of God's divine plan. 6 I am in harmony with God's kingdom within me and around me. 7 I can discern when I am tempted by my error thoughts, and I pray to God for release. 8 I turn my consciousness towards God's love so that I may distance myself from falsehoods. 9 God is my all in all; my thoughts are elevated beyond the material plane. 10 When I meditate on God's goodness I have nothing

to fear from any evil that I may encounter. 11 God's presence
shines a light upon me; I am joyful and I am comforted. 12 My
prayers are filled with gratitude as I celebrate God's grace.

My eyes cannot see God, but I am a witness to the order and chaos of creation and the laws of nature at work. I need no further proof, nor should I
expect any explanation of the incomprehensible mystery that is God. What
I know for sure, though, is that God's creative energy is infinite. It is the
kind of energy that can literally move mountains or push a tiny flower
through a crack in the sidewalk.

There are those who are blessed with a surplus of creative genius. I think
of Mozart as a child, composing complex pieces of music; of Michelangelo
creating his sculptures out of blocks of Carrara marble; of Albert Einstein
understanding relativity. Everywhere I look there are people with gifts,
working hard to benefit people and planet.

And, when tragedy strikes, I see God in a relief worker's gentle touch. I see
God when a baby is brought out alive from under rubble. I see God when
people reach out to comfort one another in the face of tremendous loss. I
don't believe that God is the source of illness or of those events that tear
at our hearts. I do believe that God is present at those times, that God is
in the midst of the worst times of our lives, always holding us gently and
with great love.

This is what I am called to do: to meditate on God's eternal love. All that
is asked is that I nurture my faith and use my gifts in ways that honor
Creation, however that may look.

PSALM 98

1 Each day it is time for a new song of thanks to God for all the wonders of creation; God sends Spirit throughout heaven and earth to bring love and goodness. 2 God offers the gift of redemption to the faithful and to those who seek to do good. 3 God's love encompasses all people, but those whose spiritual consciousness is lifted up will feel it first. 4 Sing songs with a powerful voice, be joyful and make music. 5 The vibrations of singing will bring harmony and healing to body, mind and spirit; 6 that same harmony fills every cell with delight. 7 From the deeps of the oceans the whales sing; the earth's creatures each have their anthems. 8 The rivers will roar over the rocks and the mountains will echo the refrains; 9 this symphony plays to announce the glory of God manifested throughout the earth.

Psalm 98 encourages me to celebrate life through the making of music. I am to raise my voice in song, use whatever instrument I have, and send the notes into the ether.

I wonder how and when the human voice was first used to assemble the sounds that make music and what it felt like to send those sounds into the cosmos. Or, when did someone imagine that a hollow reed with holes made in it would produce a pleasing noise? Or that blowing into a ram's horn could gather people together in worship?

I periodically visit the Benedictine monastery in Northern New Mexico. It is situated down 13 miles of rough forest service road among some of the most breathtaking scenery in New Mexico. The monks at Christ In the

Desert monastery use a simple chant to hold the words of the Psalms as they are sent from the chapel into the pure desert air. Just a few notes are employed. There is no harmony, no back-up singers, no trumpets or cymbals to help carry the message. The result is a combination of sound and word that is elegant in its simplicity.

For me, music has the power to take me straight to God. Singing in church may be my most treasured activity. Every care and worry subsides for the few minutes that melody and harmony sound in my head and my soul. I thank God for bringing me into the presence of music, for enfolding me with sounds and rhythms, for giving me ears to hear and a voice to harmonize. May it always be so. Go Altos!

PSALM 99

1 God is absolute, we are humbled in God's presence; angels carry God's message of truth to those who listen. 2 Where God is, love abides; there is no greater source of good. 3 Words of praise and thanksgiving lead us to spiritual wholeness. 4 God gives strength to those who work for justice and equality; through God they receive inspiration for their efforts. 5 Worship God and come into God's presence; pray for wholeness of spirit. 6 Pray to God to find awareness of God within, and spiritual discernment grows in strength; in the silence we learn of God's wisdom. 7 Enter the silence with trust that God will be found; pray and meditate on God's truth. 8 Pray for newness of thought and Spirit will answer; false claims will lose their power and righteousness will prevail. 9 Pray for greater awareness of God's will, and give thanks for God's glory.

Psalm 99 brings out the importance of approaching God in whatever way we can, through prayer and meditation and a willingness to go within to a sacred place. In the Bible, the prophets seemed to be especially attuned to hear the voice of God, or to experience God through other senses.

I have had moments when I felt an intimate connection with God. I have heard, not God's voice, but God's words through the wisdom of others around me. I have felt a close proximity to God through my encounters with people, or in the midst of this earth's wild places.

Psalm 99 brings to mind James Dillet Freeman's Prayer for Protection:

"The Light of God surrounds us. The Love of God enfolds us. The Power of God protects us. The Presence of God watches over us. Wherever we are, God IS...and all is well!"

PSALM 100

A psalm. For giving grateful praise.

1 Shouts of acclamation ring throughout Creation. 2 Gratitude and joy spring forth from prayers sent out to God. 3 Divine Mind shapes substance and makes the earth and all that live upon it; God's love extends to all creatures. 4 There is no better way to show our love for God than by speaking words of thanksgiving and praise; we come into God's presence with grateful hearts. 5 God's goodness and love know no end; God is with us through all our generations.

We enter into mosques, synagogues, cathedrals, temples and sanctuaries praying to God to be guided by holy wisdom. Language may differ, spaces may reflect a difference in how we honor God, the sources of our holiest teachings will vary, the ways that we sit or kneel are taught to us early on, but we are all speaking to the Source that gives us life.

In addition to the gift of life, I believe that God sends us each to this life with a tiny built in God-spark of joy. Babies know about discomfort, and crying is a message to an adult to soothe whatever the source may be. But the predominant aura of a baby is one of joy. Holding a baby is an opportunity to experience the grace and happiness of God's creation. I wish that the world treasured innocence and delight more than it does. Life would be simpler and happier then!

PSALM 101

Of David. A psalm.

1 My daily prayers will be hymns of praise and thanksgiving for your love. 2 My intention is to live with care for all your creation – how can I not see you there? Your inspiration is all I need to live a clean life. 3 I will look for the good that surrounds me. My faith will not be shaken; I will live according to your truth. 4 If I am in the presence of evil, I will deny its power over me. 5 I will not take part in speaking ill of others; if my pride whispers to me I will deny its power over me. 6 My teachers will be people of faith and I will study their wisdom; I will follow the one who is filled with love and good works. 7 I will live with honesty as a guide; if untruth surrounds me I will deny its power over me. 8 I will meditate every day on

*God's goodness; I will seek the company of those who live with
integrity in their hearts.*

Psalm 101 is written in present and future tense. It is a reminder that innocence and an open heart set a tone for my day-to-day life. Living in God's
grace, seeking a merciful outlook, opening my heart and mind to God's
loving presence. These are all practices that lead to a peaceful soul. And,
they are conscious choices that require discipline and a steady conviction
to do the next right thing.

Choose to think positively, to look for the good. Choose to avoid rancor and
gossip. Choose the high road, even if it takes work to get there. Commit to
let go of that which attracts negativity. Learn new ways to deal with conflict, because there is no escaping it. If I would practice these every day I
would go a long way toward keeping my life simple and true.

PSALM 102

**A prayer of an afflicted person who has grown weak
and pours out a lament before the LORD.**

*1 God, I call out to you because I need your healing power. 2
I am afflicted and I pray for relief. I need strength of spirit
to enter into the silence and seek you; I ask for your calm-
ing presence. 3 My days pass away as though they are not
real; my body burns with distress. 4 My heart feels empty and
closed to your love; I have no need of food for nourishment.
5 My pleas to you are mere whispers and my body is fading
away. 6 Whatever wisdom I had is ebbing away, and I am
too exhausted to pursue it. 7 Sleep eludes me; I am alone in*

the night. 8 In the daylight I am haunted by my ills; no one can comfort me. 9 When I eat, I taste dust; my tears are my drink 10 because I have drawn away from you and I am lost. 11 Even the daylight seems dark to me and I fear the coming of night. 12 I long to know you again, God, for your presence has always been within me and around me. 13 I have felt your love and I have been exalted; open me, God, so that I may be filled with your love again. 14 I am a slave to this illness; I have given myself over to it. 15 I pray for relief from these thoughts of negativity; I pray for guidance from Spirit. 16 Only you can lift me up, God, and restore me. 17 Come to me when I am in the silence; hear my plea for help. 18 I will tell others that you raised me off this bed and they will know your Truth. 19 I will tell of your healing, that in the midst of my prayers you gave me an answer, 20 and that my body was released from afflic-tion. 21 I will praise your name and lift it up for others to hear and know that you elevated my thoughts 22 out of the realm of sickness; they will know of your healing powers. 23 Do not let me give in to this weakness that leads to certain death. 24 I will pray: "God, I ask for strength of spirit so that I may overcome and feel alive again. I long to live out my appointed days. 25 Your love and goodness transformed substance into this world that I know; even the stars are your creations. 26 The divine energy that gave me life will continue beyond my last breath; I will be changed. 27 But your love is eternal and you do not have an ending. 28 Restore in me the innocence and trust with which I was born; then I will live to praise you."

Psalm 102 is one of the seven "penitential" psalms. The poet is clearly in distress as his illness consumes his body and corrodes his soul. Why the writer has been plagued with this disease is not made clear. There is no mention of wrongdoing, or sinning, that might lead the writer to make a connection between devastating illness and some past action. Yet, there are so many people who look upon disaster as some kind of divine retribution.

God does not practice retaliation, because, as Unity teaches me, God is all love and goodness. Thoughts of a vengeful God lead to feelings of fear and alienation, which is an untenable state of being. Prayer and meditation open me to God's mercy, and I am comforted. God is always with me, always loving, always compassionate. Recognizing this, believing it at my deepest level, brings me peace of mind, body and soul.

And yet, suffering exists, despite our pleas. Whenever I read Psalm 102 my friend, Kemet, rises from my memory. Kemet, who died on the mesa near Abiquiu, New Mexico, wondering if he had finished his work; Kemet, the artist whose soul was bound with the ancient ones so that his brush could tell their story; Kemet, whose visions of God were expressed through the shapes and colors on his canvases.

Once Kemet got the diagnosis, his death sentence, really, he held his fears close to him and rarely spoke them out loud. Whether or not he spoke to God is a mystery to me, and the answer doesn't matter. The evidence of his passionate relationship with his creator is revealed through his works of art and through his music.

All I know for sure is this: he had the ability to create beauty and power on a blank canvas. His talent lived in his imagination and he brought it to life. This was his gift from God, evidence of God's grace moving through an open soul, who in turn gave his gift to those who knew him. Kemet was a chosen one. This I believe. That he was called back so soon is a piece of the mystery that is beyond my understanding.

PSALM 103

Of David.

1 I give thanks to God and from the deepest place in me, I am grateful. 2 I praise God for all the blessings that come to me – 3 I bring my distress to God in prayer and my mind is eased 4 and my thoughts are turned towards love and mercy. 5 I am refreshed while praying and my meditation brings me inspiration. 6 I am led to work for justice as I follow God's direction. 7 As I spend time in meditation, my spirit reaches out for God's wisdom: 8 I learn to turn my anger into compassion, and to lead from a place of love. 9 I learn about patience and the blessing of understanding; 10 for there is little benefit to dwelling with anger. 11 God's love extends throughout the universe; 12 it is God's love that brings forgiveness of my iniquities. 13 As a child responds to a parent's love, so I am led to believe in God's overarching care; 14 for God is the source of all life; God breathes life into me at my very beginning. 15 I am given my days to live by careful use of God's abundance; 16 I live day by day and pray to use my time wisely, so that I may be remembered for acts of kindness. 17 The energy of life is never ending, supported by God's love that passes from parent to child – 18 I was taught to study God's laws and live by them. 19 The realm of Divine Mind is open to me when I pray and meditate. 20 I have much to be grateful for, and more lessons to learn. 21 I raise my prayers to God and I feel the presence of Spirit. 22 God's abundance is evident wherever I look, throughout creation there is always enough. For that I am grateful.

Psalm 103 reads like a gratitude prayer, where the poet spells out all of the reasons for me to be filled with thanks for God's abundant grace. The poet writes of the qualities of mercy and compassion that God freely gives. God gives them to me and, in return, I can best honor God by making them my touchstones.

Forgiveness is another quality that comes with careful reflection and prayer. Despite my flaws and my shortcomings, God is merciful toward me. It seems only right that, in return, I make every effort to extend that same mercy to my fellow travelers. This means that I must temper my tendency to judge, to assume that I know the breadth of someone else's big picture. I think about this saying: "Everyone you meet is fighting a battle you know nothing about. Be kind."

When I read this psalm I am led into a state of awe of God's omnipresence. In many psalms, the words "fear God" are used. I prefer to substitute the word "awe" in place of fear. Awe allows me to have the greatest respect for God and for Creation. Awe invokes wonder, reverence, and a strong desire to live my best life. Awe allows for self-reflection in order to live into God's covenant with me. Awe means living with my eyes wide open so that I can take it all in and make every effort to give it all back.

PSALM 104

1 I give thanks to God with body, mind, and soul; God is the ultimate creator of All That Is on earth and in the heavens.
2 Spiritual understanding comes from the light of God's

presence; this light is eternal 3 and available to all whose inner eye is open to see it. 4 Angels bring God's messages when they are most needed, and the cleansing fire of Spirit accompanies them. 5 With our senses we study the material world that appears as a solid foundation. 6 With our subconscious mind we intuit God's word and our contemplation leads us to good works. 7 But we must guard against a flood of negative thoughts, for they bring uncertainty and doubt; 8 they cause our ideals to fade, to be forgotten. 9 But when God's goodness is sought, negativity recedes. 10 God's abundance overflows throughout creation. 11 It brings food and drink and shelter to all creatures; no one is denied. 12 Even the smallest bird will build a nest and feel safe in God's wild places. 13 Living water quenches a thirsty spirit; God's word nourishes the soul. 14 Substance is manifested as abundance – there is enough for all: 15 those who wish to fill themselves with God's goodness will be sustained. 16 As the roots of strong trees search for water, so do we enter into the silence seeking communion with God. 17 There we are able to affirm our truth and measure it against God's divine truth. 18 Our thoughts are elevated into the spiritual realm and we are secure in Spirit's presence. 19 God's wisdom is found in the light and the darkness. 20 When we are troubled and our spirits are in darkness, 21 when our strength begins to ebb, we turn to God. 22 God's light shines for us and we are refreshed. 23 When we have done God's work and are in need of rest, we meditate. 24 God's labors never end, for creation is always in need of God's love and goodness. 25 Divine Mind is the source of endless designs – the substance of dreams yet unseen. 26 Whoever enters the silence to meditate opens the door to understanding the *vastness of God's creation. 27 Communion with God through prayer brings spiritual enlightenment. 28 God's abundance is manifest to those who trust in God's divine plan. 29 False thoughts and error behaviors can be changed and redeemed while seeking God's wisdom. 30 Spirit comes to us and we are made whole. 31 God is omnipresence and omniscience; there is no end to God's creation. 32 God's laws create the stars in the heavens, and send fire from the mountaintops. 33 I will sing my praise to God now and forever. 34 The words that I offer God come from a place of deepest awe. 35 I pray only that God's goodness may touch all hearts. My soul sings with love for God and my words are hymns to God's glory.*

The miracles of creation shine through the words of Psalm 104. We have had centuries since these words were written to search for rational, scientific explanations of the phenomena described by the poet. With probing minds we invent instruments that extend our gifts of sight and hearing and understanding. Now we look at creation on a sub-molecular level. We have photographs of distant stars and galaxies and they are only a tiny portion of an unending universe. We look into the cells whose walls hold life, evidence that we live in a complex web woven from inanimate materials that somehow combine to become animate beings. We live in a world that relies on cycles: day and night, high tides and low tides, changing seasons, phases of our moon, and our very own life transitions. This is all the proof I need that there is a Holy Wisdom at work in us and around us.

PSALM 105

1 It is always time to give thanks to God; to make known God's creative powers. 2 God can be praised in song, or in words that tell of the miracles of creation. 3 Celebrate God's wisdom and honor those who follow it. 4 In God's presence, spirits are upheld; enter the silence with God. 5 Learn of God's abundance and the wonders of God's achievements, 6 for we are God's children, and we are people of faith searching for spiritual enlightenment. 7 God is omnipresence; God is omniscience. 8 We make a commitment to God to do good works as long as we are able; 9 we enter into it with faith and we are at peace. 10 God is at work within us, lifting our spirits to greater understanding. 11 We are ready to learn and we are humble before God. 12 When we face the unknown, 13 with prayer and meditation we find a way to make it known. 14 We face adversity with confidence that we have within us the power to overcome it. 15 We go to the source of our spiritual strength and in our prayer we speak words of truth. 16 When we fear lack and deprivation, 17 we have only to imagine that what we need lies before us, 18 and we release the thoughts that bind us. 19 We study God's word and we learn that we are enough. 20 We meditate on our good fortune and we are set free. 21 Spirit's presence reminds us that we are capable of doing great things with what God has given us. 22 We speak this truth without hesitation and we become teachers of God's wisdom. 23 If we are prisoners of our possessions we live only in sense consciousness. 24 We must then turn to God and ask that our spiritual understanding be magnified, 25 so that we may overcome the limiting thoughts of material gain. 26 We seek to raise our thinking beyond the earth plane and we move toward a greater understanding of Spirit. 27 We pray that any doubts be erased. 28 If we enter a place of darkness we meditate on its meaning – do we not know that God will answer? 29 Then we are open to receive spiritual principles that will raise us up. 30 Our error thoughts are quieted, no matter their number. 31 Though we are tempted by external trappings we can overcome this. 32 We are given the understanding that spiritual enlightenment is within us when we commune with God. 33 Our minds become sources of enlightenment and our spirits flourish. 34 When we are in a swarm of troubling thoughts, we have only to go within to find peace; 35 we need not give in to any distress that devours our faith. 36 When faced with the greatest threat, we pray and we affirm the power of God's protection. 37 We go to our source of love and wisdom and we are given strength. 38 We will show our gratitude for God's presence by performing good works. 39 God is a never-ending source of comfort and peace, even in the darkest night. 40 God's abundance brings us what we need when we are open to receive it. 41 If we are thirsty, God's living water quenches us. 42 Our faith is strengthened when we trust in God. 43 All people receive God's blessing; 44 everyone is a child of God − 45 may God's love wash over all people. Praise God.

Psalm 105 is a prayer about having and keeping a covenant with God. In the traditional version the poet who wrote this one used it as an opportunity to condense history, to write about Israel's bondage in Egypt, and to tell of God's subsequent actions to set people free. The story and the people involved in it can be interpreted according to Unity thought. By using the *Metaphysical Bible Dictionary* I am given the deeper meanings of this well-known biblical story. Abraham is a man of faith; Moses draws forth Spirit; Aaron is a source of increasing spiritual strength; Isaac is the joy of spiritual consciousness.

Reading Psalm 105 with Unity principles in mind makes it very clear for me that I have a relationship with God because I am of God. I have a responsibility to maintain my interconnection with God and Spirit through the use of denials and affirmations and the practices of prayer and meditation.

Thinking back, I can chart my spiritual evolution over the years. I grew up in a house where religion was not practiced or discussed. Not until I got to college and took a course in Eastern religions were my spiritual eyes opened. I began to sing in my college chapel choir and so I was introduced to words of faith set to music. I joined a church in my 30s because the minister's sermons helped me understand how to apply the Bible's teachings to my daily life. In my early 60s I discovered Unity and immediately felt at home. As I see it now, my spiritual development may very well resemble the journey that Israel took from bondage to freedom!

PSALM 106

1 We are called to give thanks to God, whose divine plan is bound by love and goodness. 2 Who among us can describe the extent of God's Creation? 3 Those who study God's laws are committed to live with justice and right actions as their foundation. 4 May I be remembered as one who sought counsel from God, 5 one who honored God's abundance, one who freely praised God. 6 We continue to give in to error thoughts and false claims; we have not learned to forsake them. 7 Lessons from our past remain obscure to us; we live in sense consciousness. 8 God is present everywhere, as close as the next breath. 9 Knowing this, we give up our limited ways and look for the guidance that God provides. 10 Being in communion with God can be our salvation; our freedom from the bondage of error thinking. 11 God, as Divine Mind, invites us to consider absolute truth. 12 God's Word strengthens our faith. 13 But in our weakness we can quickly forget what God holds for us. 14 When we find ourselves in a barren place we need Spirit's guidance to lead us out. 15 Spiritual riches can be ours until we confuse pride with piety. 16 The way out of error is through prayer, acknowledging that we need spiritual instruction to reach a new state of consciousness. 17 Our rites and ceremonies are not enough to make way for spiritual growth. 18 We need the purifying energy of Spirit to cleanse our thoughts. 19 Rather than worship false idols we must enter the silence with God. 20 Only in that sacred space will we overcome material thinking. 21 Even though we set aside the evidence of God's abundance, 22 it is always there for those who rise above sense consciousness. 23 We call upon Spirit to lead us upward in our thinking. 24 There are those who deny God's abundance; they do not believe in it. 25 They choose thoughts of lack and deprivation and their unhappiness increases. 26 They bring unease upon themselves, 27 and upon all those who listen to them. 28 They believe only in that which their senses demonstrate to them; 29 they worship false idols and forsake God's teachings. 30 Only when their thoughts awaken to matters of spirit are they released from uncertainty. 31 Then there is no end to the spiritual riches that can come to them. 32 Then can sense consciousness be overcome, and the work of Spirit can begin. 33 There is no room for doubt and negativity while seeking God's counsel. 34 We can learn to live among those who think differently about God and Spirit for we are all children of God. 35 We must not be trapped by negative thoughts. 36 Nor should we give in to

the allure of false idols. 37 That surely leads to spiritual pov-
erty. 38 Then the realm of pure ideals is not open to us. 39
Our actions will not be founded in God's goodness and mercy.
40 We draw farther and farther away from God. 41 Material
goods rule over our consciousness. 42 Error thoughts fill our
minds and we become as slaves to them. 43 God and Spirit
hold so many opportunities for us to escape this bondage. 44
All we need is to pray for release and meditate on God's good-
ness; 45 for God's love is always available to those who seek it.
46 God's mercy and forgiveness are ever present. 47 We need
only ask for it, and pray that we may encounter Spirit's divine
energy. 48 We shall be grateful for God's redemptive power
and give thanks and praise to God.

Psalm 106 is similar to Psalm 105 in that it continues the story of people led out of slavery and to a new life in a different land. It is a history psalm that tells of God's enduring patience with a fractious, disobedient, and willful people who "tested" God at every turn. They became practicing hedonists, expecting to be given whatever they wanted, whenever they wanted it.

For me, Psalm 106 is a painful reminder of the range of human faults, collective and personal. We, I, so easily stray from living in gratitude. I am prone to looking for an easier way through any adversity. This short-sighted, immediate gratification tendency has at times ruled my life. This is absolutely when I am most prone to make poor choices and start dusting off my false idols. In my mind, I rationalize that the idol will bring me comfort. I have learned the hard way that the idol offers no real consolation. It remains still, and cold, standing in the distance with no real interest in those who worship at its feet. Sadly, I have built many an altar to false promises that are nothing but a convenient barrier to honest self appraisal.

As I worked with Psalm 106, I was reminded that spiritual discipline is the key to overcoming unproductive, self-serving behaviors.

Chapter Six

BOOK V

Psalms 107 – 150

PSALM 107

1 It is always time to be grateful for God's goodness and love; it is there for everyone. 2 Those who know God speak words of enlightenment – words that instruct others in God's ways. 3 These people are found throughout the earth, from every direction. 4 They speak from a place of deep knowledge, having come through difficult times with God's guidance. 5 They have known hunger and poverty of spirit, they have been in great distress. 6 They meditated with great care, entering the silence and seeking God's wisdom. 7 God was with them as they sought release from their troubles, and they were comforted. 8 Now they give thanks always for God's blessings, 9 they are filled with God's spiritual food. 10 Some were alone and without confidence, bound by hopelessness, 11 unwilling to open themselves to God's wisdom. 12 In their quest to find an easier way, they suffered and found no relief. 13 They came to God, bereft and uncertain, and God's enduring love began to flow through them. 14 Spirit taught them to pray, and their darkness was lifted. 15 Now they give thanks always for God's blessings, 16 and in their meditations, they release the error thoughts that had filled them. 17 Some were too arrogant and closely bound to sense thinking and had no interest in finding God inside of them. 18 They refused to consider God's abundant goodness and were filled with thoughts of lack. 19 Spirit led them to meditate with great care, to enter the silence and seek God's wisdom. 20 They learned of God's healing love and they were released from their bondage. 21 Now they give thanks always for God's blessings. 22 They renounced their old beliefs and they were filled with joy. 23 They went forth seeking Divine Mind; they were lifted up into a higher spiritual consciousness. 24 Their prayers and meditations took them deeper into Wisdom. 25 God's Word stirred their souls and they were comforted. 26 But some refused God's counsel and they continued in their material consciousness. 27 They wandered aimlessly, with no sense of spiritual direction, 28 until, in their desperation, they called out for God's help. 29 They prayed to God and were given a sense of peace; their souls were tranquil. 30 They knew that they were safe, that their prayers were being answered. 31 Now they give thanks always for God's blessings. 32 They spoke of God's goodness and love wherever there were people who would listen. 33 They said that God's living water will quench even the greatest thirst. 34 They spoke to those who were filled with doubt, and gave them hope. 35 God's goodness prevailed among them; 36 those who hungered for deeper communion with God were satisfied. 37 They called upon their centers of consciousness

and they found greater faith. 38 They also reached higher lev-
els of thought that lead to spiritual richness. 39 The spiritually
enlightened cannot be brought back down into sense con-
sciousness for they have learned the greatest lesson. 40 They
know that God's abundance is always present and available
when their thoughts affirm it. 41 Their afflictions fade away
when they are denied and replaced with positive thoughts. 42
They see with spiritual eyes and they know happiness. 43 They
are wise examples of God's love and grace.

Psalm 107 is a study in the availability of God's mercy. All that is required is a willingness to seek holy guidance. Psalm107 speaks of different groups of people who are alienated from God by choice. What the people all have in common is their willingness at some point to enter into communion with God and to seek a different way of living and thinking. This is freedom at work in that we are each able to exercise our free will and make decisions that lead us out of whatever bondage we have created for ourselves.

I know by now that the choices I make lead me into light or into darkness. I have reflected on this many times, seeing in retrospect how my will has led me to places that are not good for me. I can remember times when I have been lost, or imprisoned in my own mind, or foolish beyond belief, or standing at the edge of catastrophe. In my sometimes clumsy prayers I have asked for God's help, gotten it, and lived to tell about it.

For the spiritually hungry, for those in a prison of their own making, for those plagued by doubt, for those who are lonely, there is comfort to be found in Psalm 107. It is not an easy comfort. It requires a discipline of mind and soul. It requires a commitment to an honest search for redemption from error thinking and a willingness to make changes. It calls for patience, and an ability to discern how much is mine to carry, and how much is truly beyond my control.

PSALM 108

A song. A psalm of David

1 You, God, are at the very depth of my being; I sing only songs of gratitude. 2 You are there when I awaken as the dawn fades into day. 3 My words will praise you, my songs will tell of your abundance. 4 Your love moves the stars in the heavens; and it watches over a beating heart. 5 Your love raises our consciousness to a higher plane of thought; your goodness covers all creation. 6 Lead us into your precious silence so that we may come close to you and learn of your faithfulness. 7 We seek your word so that we may walk upright in your light and abide as spiritual beings. 8 We seek a higher consciousness and better understanding; through affirmations we will raise our ideals. 9 Your thoughts are only of goodness; you teach us to honor our physical bodies and to train our senses to seek your good. 10 You will show us the spiritual center of our consciousness. 11 God, you will never turn against us for you come from the place of purest love. 12 We seek your wisdom to keep us from sense ignorance. 13 Through you we will attain spiritual discipline and enlightenment.

Psalm 108 appears to have been cobbled together using parts of Psalms 57 and 60. Nevertheless, it is a prayer from a faithful person, extolling God's goodness and God's protection. It is a psalm whose words I can use as paths to travel on while seeking a closer relationship with God. I rely on its ancient wisdom to remind me that God lives within me. I use this prayer to reach out to God when my own words fail me.

Unity teaches me that God, Divine Mind, dwells within. There are many ways to reach God, music being one of them. When I sing, I feel like I am on a path to the divine. In *The Revealing Word*, Charles Fillmore says this about singing: "Singing, praising, and thanksgiving are the great building impulses of man. Never repress the desire to give thanks through happy songs and words of praise. Singing restores harmony to tense nerves because its vibrations stir them to action, thus making it possible for the ever-waiting, healing Spirit to get in."[47]

PSALM 109

For the director of music. Of David. A psalm.

1 God, I call to you in my distress, and I need your wisdom, 2 because people I trusted have betrayed me; they speak of me with words that are not true. 3 What they say about me is hurtful; they have no reason to speak in this way. 4 Who I thought were friends are not after all, and I can only pray about this. 5 But because of you, God, I can turn away from their malevolence, I do not need to give in to it. 6 I will come to you for guidance and I will not fear their words. 7 It is not for me to judge them for their actions are not mine. 8 I will not spend my days thinking of them, for I do not need their counsel. 9 Whatever befalls them is not of my making. 10 IF they are poor in spirit I pray that they will know peace. 11 If they are tied to their material needs, I pray that they may

---

47   Fillmore, Charles, *The Revealing Word*, 180.

have enough. 12 If I encounter them I will look upon them with kindness. 13 I will not follow their ways today or tomorrow and I will put them behind me. 14 Whatever they have learned from their ancestors, it is not my lesson. 15 I do not need to be led by their error thinking. 16 If I witness their unkind ways I pray that they may be released from their fears. 17 When their harmful words come into my awareness I will not give them any importance and I will be free from their ire. 18 If they utter profanity I will not absorb it into my being. 19 I will continue to pray for their release from disrespect of others. 20 Rather than carry this trouble with me I will meditate on the best way to rise above it. 21 I know that there are lessons for me to learn and I will enter the silence and pray to you, God. 22 For I carry my own faults with me, and I need to be cleansed by Spirit's purifying fire. 23 If not, I will fall prey to my own negative thoughts. 24 I will pray that my spirit is not weakened by the antagonism of the people who might wish me ill. 25 I will pray that kindness will be my attitude. 26 I will meditate and seek your counsel, God. 27 I will pray that others may also know your love and your goodness. 28 If they speak ill of you, bless them; if they speak ill of me I will do the same. 29 If they cannot see the goodness in your creation I will pray that their blinders be removed. 30 I will praise God for all of the good works that come from God; I will raise my voice in praise. 31 For God is my foundation in the presence of all troubles.

Betrayal is painful. When it has happened to me I have trouble envisioning God in the middle of its murkiness, but perhaps that is the best place in which to search for God's wisdom. When my sense of justice and fairness is turned upside down and outrage takes its place I sometimes have trouble seeing clearly past my personal vision of the wrong being done. I have learned through experience that betrayal is most often about looking within the circumstances to find the lesson that I am meant to learn. If I feel that I have been betrayed, I need to examine the whole cloth and find the threads that are mine.

Unity teaches me that holding on to rancor only brings more of it to me. I learn the value of the power of forgiveness that is far more useful than any efforts to repay negativity with more of the same. My other lesson was learned from a sweet friend of mine who is no longer with us in this world. My friend's default mode in the face of someone who troubled her was to pray for that person. I will always remember that quality about her. She taught me that this action of praying for someone who is causing me distress requires mindfulness and a loving heart. She also taught me another valuable lesson: it is far more important to do the next right thing than it is to be right.

PSALM 110

Of David. A psalm.

1 When I enter the silence to hear God's words, any worries that I have melt away. 2 My heart is eased by entering love's abode, and my understanding of God's will for me grows. 3 My thoughts develop and take form as I meditate. They come to life as I affirm God's presence. 4 God's wisdom, which never changes, leads me toward a place of peace and perfection. 5 God is with me no matter what I encounter. 6 There is nothing to fear because my body, mind, and spirit are under God's protection. 7 God's abundance brings me everything I need and I am strengthened.

In its original form, Psalm 110 is written in preparation for a battle. I have struggled with this one for years, especially in the context of troops of young people sent out to a certain death for some of them. This is an "Of David" psalm, and I suppose that, being a warrior king, his thoughts and prayers reflected a warrior's worries and hopes.

There are times when I do battle with my own life. With nowhere else to turn, fresh out of ideas and options, with no plans to move me forward, I am apt to forget about my strongest ally until I am stopped in my tracks. Thankfully, that is the time when I am finally wise enough to ask God for direction. I do not like to admit that I am vulnerable, but there is something cleansing about that realization.

Unity teaches me that I can approach God whenever I want, wherever I am. Be it through prayer, or meditation, or both, answers surely appear. My lesson is to remember that I need to pay attention.

"Prayer is more than supplication. It is an affirmation of Truth that eternally exists, but which has not yet come into consciousness. It comes into consciousness not by supplication but by affirmation."[48]

PSALM 111

1 To praise God is to show gratitude for God's goodness. I will give thanks in word and in song and I will honor God's

---

48   Fillmore, Charles, *The Revealing Word*, 152.

presence. 2 God's creation is absolute and eternal; all who revere its design are uplifted. 3 God's love brings into being the universe and all that it contains; divine love is boundless. 4 Through faith we are reminded that God is merciful to all of creation's children. 5 Those who honor God learn that God's will for us is always for our highest good. 6 Those who rely on God's abundance will have all that they need. 7 God's powers never waver; God's infinite laws promote justice and uphold the innocent. 8 They do not change, they exist for the good of all beings. 9 When I enter the silence, I honor my covenant with God – to follow God's truth in all that I do. 10 A spiritual clarity about God's wisdom is found through prayer and meditation. Praise God in all ways.

Throughout the ten verses of Psalm 111 I am reminded again and again that when I am conscious of God's manifestations I am rich in spirit. From the Higgs Boson to the complexity of the universe there are infinite bits of information to be accessed. May I seek those that help me to be a better steward of my place in creation.

Faith tells me that when I turn myself toward thoughts of truth and fairness I can make a commitment to practice them to the best of my ability. God's wisdom, greater than my imagining can comprehend, is always available to me. When I pray, I can ask God for the perseverance and discipline to look beyond what I think I know, and measure my thoughts and actions using God's gifts as my guide. Only then will I be most likely to serve God in ways that honor God's manifestations.

PSALM 112

1 Give thanks to God. Those who approach God with reverence will be blessed, and they will follow God's call with joy. 2 They will be strong in spirit; they will always choose justice. 3 They will be blessed with abundance, and they will use it for good purposes. 4 Even in the midst of sorrow they will find comfort, for they understand mercy and compassion. 5 They will share what they have and practice justice and fairness. 6 Their lives are secure, and they know of God's enduring love. 7 When distress brushes against them they will seek God's consolation. 8 Their foundation is love and they affirm the presence of Spirit; they will live with grace. 9 They affirm the power of giving; they approach others with love; they devote their lives to good purposes. 10 Therefore, they do not know shame or iniquity; they only know the blessings of faithfulness.

When I read Psalm 112 I am certain that I want to be a person who follows in the ways of mercy and love. I want to open all my senses to God's Truth. Unity tells me that God and I are inseparable, and that through prayer and meditation and discernment I can reach a greater understanding of that bond.

I want to be a generous person, and the older I get, the easier that is for me. In my younger days, possessions meant a lot. To be honest, on occasion I still have to use discipline and discernment to avoid the trap of trappings. This comes from an old place of fear that I would not have "enough." It has taken me many years to reach a more Zen state of mind that allows me to accept that more often than not, less is more.

Unity teaches me that prosperity is not just about wealth and possessions. It is, instead, a state of mind that encourages me to give freely and to receive with gratitude. I am led into a "prosperity consciousness" with the belief that God's abundance is everywhere. God, Divine Mind, has filled the universe with substance out of which material things manifest. This is what underlies true prosperity. As I reflect on thoughts of abundance, knowing that it is everywhere, I become secure in the belief that there is always ENOUGH. I can change my fears of lack into affirmations about the best way to use my prosperity.

PSALM 113

1 Praise God. All those who follow God's law, praise God; speak God's name with reverence. 2 For all things, give thanks to Divine Mind that exists for all eternity. 3 Thank God for the light of day and the soothing darkness of night. 4 God is in every part of creation, on earth and in the skies. 5 Who can doubt God's presence and power, 6 knowing that God's love is in all that is, seen and unseen? 7 The poor in spirit can enter the silence and learn of God's wisdom and those in need can find abundance; 8 communion with God lifts the spirit out of despair. 9 Those who study God's precepts shall be nurtured and will know joy. Praise God.

Psalm 113 begins a series of six praise psalms, each one encouraging the faithful to always give thanks and praise God. If I spent the rest of my life discovering ways to live out this short command, I would not have time to practice all of its permutations. I wonder then if it is possible to train for this challenge much as a runner trains to run a marathon. It's a commitment of time and energy and singleness of purpose. It calls for careful consideration of next steps, like a climber on a tricky slope or a hiker on an unmarked trail. I certainly need guides along the way. Here, I need to stop a moment and give heartfelt thanks for the people who have been my shepherds over the years!

To praise God is to open my mind to consider all of the reasons why giving thanks can be so powerful. The psalm tells us that God is in and around everything, giving all people the opportunity to express gratitude and, in so doing, be in relationship with God. There is no special place in which to do this because wherever I am, God is within and around me.

PSALM 114

1 When we are bound to sense consciousness God offers freedom, 2 and through prayer and praise we are united with Spirit. 3 We are invited to enter the realm of Divine Mind and cleanse the streams of thoughts that do not serve us; 4 in doing so, our thoughts are elevated beyond the material plane. 5 Why do we not always seek to increase our spiritual consciousness? 6 Why do we not rein in our scattered thoughts and bring them to bear on thanks and praise? 7 Our bodies tremble as we encounter the I AM, 8 and we drink of God's living waters.

Believing that God and Moses led the Israelites out of bondage, we can examine our own "exodus" stories. How have I managed to grow beyond my self-imposed limitations and begin a new venture? Who, or what, has led me to seek a different path? Why have I left behind a comfortable situation to try something new? Where are those places in my life when I have changed course with boldness and courage?

A form of exodus has been with us since the beginning of our evolution as a species. How else would we have made our mark on a world much wider than Mother Africa? Was it a sense of adventure, or a scarcity of resources that drove the first venture beyond the familiar? When did curiosity take hold, or necessity make boldness? From Stone Age to Bronze Age we took what we could forage and experimented until rocks became tools and fire opened a new realm of possibilities. I choose to believe that throughout this evolution the presence of God was in and around our ancestors. Psalm 114 is an invitation to venture into Spirit's domain and trust that there is only good to be found there.

PSALM 115

1 It is always good to praise God, our source of love from whom we learn the power of faith. 2 There are some who ask, "Where is God?". 3 We answer that God is both within us and around us; Divine Mind, God, is the source of all creation. 4 There are some who follow false claims, without regard for God's love and wisdom. 5 They speak only of material gains, and they do not see the glory in God's creation. 6 They do not receive the guidance of Spirit, nor do they use their senses to explore God's living world. 7 They are rooted in material consciousness and they do not speak of spiritual enlightenment. 8 They do not enter the silence to commune with God, nor do they approach the faithful ones. 9 Then there are people who live to be spiritual beings, and they rely on God as the source of life. 10 They seek a higher state of consciousness, and they rely on God as the source of life. 11 They approach God with great reverence, and they rely on God as the source of life. 12 There is not one who is not a child of God, able to receive God's blessing. 13

Those who come to God with awe in their hearts are blessed –
God's love is expansive. 14 Through prayer and affirmations
our lives are enriched. 15 The creator of All That Is surrounds
us with love and abundance. 16 God's love is extended on earth
and throughout the heavens. 17 We are all invited to have a
part in God's community as we pass through this life. 18 For
this we are grateful, now and forever. Praise God.

For me, Psalm 115 is a reminder about the vast difference between owning possessions and being owned by them. I am not so naïve as to deny that I have lived in both camps. I have made decisions that benefited my material goods more than my spiritual direction.

Unity teaches me there is always an opportunity to move beyond my rigid thinking, my idol worship, to a much broader and very freeing way of thinking and living. Unity principles help me to expand my understanding and to raise my awareness above the "sense consciousness" that binds me to unhealthy habits and selfish thoughts. Through Unity, I know I can absolutely trust God and Spirit to lead me in spiritually enriching practices. I learn this from being mindful while praying and meditating in the silence.

Every Sunday at church, there is a lovely woman who holds the "Affirmations basket" and encourages each person to take one. One Sunday when I really needed this one, here is what it said: "God is in charge, and I rely on god's law of good to bring order and justice into all areas of my life."

PSALM 116

1 When I meditate, I feel the power of God's love, and I know
that my prayers carry a message. 2 I know that God is as close

as my next breath. 3 When I was very ill and afraid for myself, distress was my companion. 4 Then I sought God's healing power and implored Spirit to stay by my side. 5 I felt the love and mercy that comes from God when I filled my mind with thoughts of health and recovery. 6 When I am unaware, both God and Spirit work in me to increase my confidence. 7 Then my soul and mind know peace, for God is with me. 8 I look back on my life and I see the times that God has protected me, 9 so that I might continue this life's journey. 10 When I meditated on my fear, God removed it; 11 I believed then in God's awesome presence and power. 12 How can I best honor God's goodness? 13 I will study God's many gifts and give thanks for them. 14 I will seek spiritual guidance in order to live a life of service. 15 I will honor the rhythm of life and death. 16 I will become a good steward of God's abundance; I will serve God with a glad heart and give thanks for spiritual richness. 17 My offering to God will be the practice of good works every day. 18 I will speak of God's love and goodness to all who will listen, 19 in the sanctuary, and I will make my house a dwelling of peace. Praise God.

This psalm is written for anyone who has ever experienced fear and uncertainty, whether from illness or from life circumstances. It is a powerful reminder of how God does not leave us. God is within us at all times.

There are so many ways in which I can acknowledge and honor God's bounty. I think of the term, "pay it forward," which speaks volumes about how to do the next right thing. There are always random acts of kindness to be done, those spontaneous gestures on behalf of another. Those can only be genuine when they come from a deep belief in the power of compassionate service.

It's impossible for life to be all goodness all the time. There is loss and fear and illness, suffering and injustice and wrongdoing, the dark sides of our humanity, and no amount of pretending ever makes them go away. Because of these difficulties, though, I have choices to make each time we encounter one another. I can always do the ostrich thing: stick my head in the sand, and hope that things will be different when I pull my head back out. Experience tells me the situation still needs resolution, and I am much better off if I pray about how to respond to the trouble with my best self.

PSALM 117

1 May all who live upon the earth give thanks to God. 2 God's love is the purest bond among all peoples, and faith in God makes all things possible. Praise God.

Psalm 117 is brief. I wonder why history has given it its own number. Perhaps it was end or the beginning of a psalm, or a surviving piece of another psalm. Or, perhaps the scribes decided that these two verses spoke for themselves and needed no further embellishment.

Nevertheless, here it is, with an important message in two verses: the God of ALL people is to praised for being the source of all possibility. Divine mercy and divine truth come from one Source!

What Unity teachings tell me is that I, too, am a source of mercy and truth, as are all beings in creation. The Divine Mind that manifests through me and around me is the same energy that brought forth the universe. It is not something I have to "find" outside of myself. It is something that dwells within and is always available if I am willing to reach for it.

Psalm 117 promises that God is a faithful lover, a legitimate soul mate, a constant in a fluctuating world. The more elaborate psalms address painful personal struggles, or visceral fears of abandonment or great loss. The poets call out for God's protection, God's attention, God's forgiveness, God's restoration of grace. Some psalms go to great lengths to record the wonders that God has manifested.

Psalm 117 simply asks that thanks be given for the two attributes of love and faithfulness that God makes available to all as we go about our daily lives.

PSALM 118

1 Praise God and give thanks for God's everlasting goodness and love. 2 Spiritual freedom comes to us through God's love. 3 Our spirits are strengthened through God's love. 4 We are filled with awe at the thought of God's love. 5 I have called to God in my distress; I was redeemed. 6 God is within me and all around me; I do not know fear. With God's protection, what can happen to me? 7 I commune with God; I am enlightened. I can overcome any obstacle. 8 I trust Divine Mind and I find comfort with God. 9 I trust Spirit and I find comfort with Spirit. 10 When trouble surrounds me I pray that I might rise above it. 11 When I am in distress, I pray that I may rise above it. 12 I have known sorrow that consumed me, but with God's help I rose above it. 13 I entered the silence to seek God's counsel. 14 I was given strength through my prayers and meditations. 15 I have known the joy of release of sense consciousness: God's wisdom has lifted me up! 16 God's wisdom and goodness sustain me at all times. 17 I am born into a new awareness of God's abiding love. 18 I have learned that my difficulties can be surmounted when I pray to God about them. 19 When I give thanks to God, my body, mind and soul are in a state of harmony. 20 I enter into this state when I meditate on my gratitude for God's gifts. 21 I am grateful for the wisdom that comes from God. 22 God is my foundation on which I build my life; 23 I am a part of God's glorious creation. 24 Each new day brings evidence of God's abundance. 25 With God's guidance I cannot fail. 26 Blessings abound in God's creation. In the sanctuary, we give thanks for our blessings. 27 We are surrounded by God's loving light, and we celebrate it. 28 We praise God and we give thanks for spiritual enlightenment. Praise God and give thanks for God's everlasting goodness and love.

Once, during a guided meditation, I was asked to imagine a location where I felt absolutely centered and safe. This was not hard for me. For most of my life, I have dreamed of such a place. It is at the edge of the sea. Two very tall rocks rise from the sand, separated by about an arm's length. The sun shines, and the rocks cast a shadow on the sand. The tide is out, so there is a dry place for me to sit between the rocks and lean against one of them. The sound of the waves brings me great peace and comfort.

If this is a place I have seen in real life, I am not aware of where or when I might have discovered it. My vision of it has a dreamlike quality, as though I have been in that place many times over eons of past experiences. All I know is it feels holy to me, as if I was there once and experienced a mystical revelation of God's presence and love.

I have not always considered that God has been and is my safety net. I know this now, with years of retrospection to back this up. So, when I reach the edge of something, I can trust I will know when to jump and when to turn around. When change portends, I am free to reflect on its meanings, to consult with a trusted advisor, to enter into prayer and meditation about it, and thus to frame my thinking with the idea of the next right thing to do. I know now that communion with God sets me in a broad place from which there are several paths.

I would really like to find my imaginary place some day.

PSALM 119

Aleph[49]

1 Those who live a life of goodness are blessed, they live according to God's law. 2 Those who study God's laws and seek God's wisdom – 3 they love justice and live accordingly. 4 God's creation is manifested through Divine Mind. 5 If only I would always follow divine principles! 6 Then I would leave remorse behind when I follow your ways. 7 In my heart I feel your love and I want to be your student. 8 I will pray for greater understanding; you will not leave me.

Beth

9 How does a youth learn about living a good life? By studying your precepts. 10 I must fill my heart with your wisdom; then I will understand your goodness. 11 I keep my prayers close to

---

49   This psalm is laid out as an acrostic, with each paragraph beginning with a letter from the Hebrew alphabet. The author writes with great devotion about all of the ways that God's love and wisdom guide us through this life.

my heart so that I will avoid error thoughts. 12 I thank you, God; open me to a better understanding of you. 13 I speak of your laws with reverence. 14 My spirit is enriched when I follow your teachings. 15 My meditations seek your guidance. 16 My heart knows joy when I study your words.

Gimel

17 Throughout my life I will learn of your goodness and I will follow your wisdom. 18 My spiritual eyes will be opened and I will see your grace. 19 When I am lost, I will find my way to you. 20 I want to learn from your precepts. 21 If I stray from your guidance I will pray for forgiveness. 22 I will be blessed when I follow your path. 23 No matter what others may think of me, I will pray and meditate in your presence. 24 My best lessons are learned in the silence with you.

Daleth

25 When I am laid low with sorrow, remind me of your constant love. 26 My prayers will be my confessions; I will learn lessons from them. 27 Open my mind to a greater insight into your words, so that my meditations lead me deeper into understanding. 28 When I am worn down with sadness, I will go to you for support. 29 May I always value honesty and may I learn to seek your Truth. 30 I follow you with faithfulness; my heart is joyful. 31 I am content to study your laws; my life will be richer for it. 32 I long to follow your ways and grow in my understanding of you.

He

33 I am your student, God, and I will keep your wisdom close until my life is over. 34 Open my mind to your precepts so that

I may follow them faithfully. 35 When I walk in your ways, God, I am lifted up. 36 My spiritual consciousness is expanded and I forget material gains. 37 May I see the richness of your creation; may I revere what is truly good for all. 38 I see your abundance and I am in awe of it. 39 If I follow your teachings, I will not know shame. 40 I long for your wisdom! When I encounter it I am blessed.

Waw

41 I am surrounded by your love, God, through it I am redeemed; 42 my faith is strengthened, for your words make me secure. 43 I want to always speak your truth, knowing that I can trust in it completely. 44 Prayer and meditation will be my teachers, and my spirit will be lifted up. 45 There is no greater freedom than to live a good life by following your wisdom. 46 I will be free to speak of your powers to any who will listen, 47 and they will know how much I love your ways. 48 I study your edicts, and I am enlightened, so that my meditations will reflect your will.

Zayin

49 I am blessed to be your servant, and I live a life filled with hope. 50 Even when I am troubled I know that I can reach you. 51 There are those who do not understand how deep my faith is and that I do not turn away from you 52 I study your creation and the laws that govern it and I am filled with comfort. 53 I look with sorrow upon those who violate creation and do not care for it. 54 I raise my voice in songs of praise wherever I am. 55 In the darkest night I know that you are in me and around me. 56 This is my strong belief: your Truth is eternal.

Heth

57 I am filled with your love, God, and I live by your words. 58 When I commune with you I am comforted; your grace is made clear to me. 59 I have examined my actions and I measure them against your wisdom. 60 I am quick to follow your example. 61 Though sometimes I am brought down by my troubles, I pray for your guidance. 62 No matter the time, I know that you are all around me and I am grateful. 63 I surround myself with people who love you and who seek your wisdom. 64 We are all enveloped in your love, God, and we learn about your mercy.

Teth

65 I rely on your goodness, God, and on your wisdom. 66 I will be your faithful student, for you are the source of inspiration. 67 In my distress I sometimes failed to seek you, but now I have faith in your words. 68 Your abundance is evident everywhere I look; may I always share what I have. 69 I do not dwell with those who doubt your presence, for I know otherwise. 70 They have hardened their hearts, but mine is filled with your love. 71 I learned of your love during a time of affliction and I have faith in your powers. 72 Your spiritual enrichment means more to me than any material goods.

Yodh

73 You made me, God; I long to understand your precepts. 74 When others see me I want them to see you. 75 Through prayer and meditation I enter a place of harmony and my faith is strengthened. 76 Your love surrounds us all and I find great comfort in it. 77 I long to practice your mercy wherever I turn. 78 Those who doubt your presence have challenged me;

but I pray for their enlightenment. 79 I will tell of your love and your teachings and seek to understand your wisdom. 80 As long as I live in harmony with creation I will have everything I need.

Kaph

81 When I contemplate your redemptive power I have hope that I may be redeemed. 82 When I am troubled I reflect on your goodness and I turn to you for comfort. 83 Though my vision may be clouded I rely on your wisdom and I seek clarity. 84 In my impatience I ask when my mind will be enlightened, and my unruly thoughts be tamed. 85 There are those who argue with me about your very existence. 86 I search my soul for the right answers to give them, but still they doubt. 87 They do not wish to learn of you, but I rely on your words that come to me when I pray. 88 I ask for your love to be manifested through me and for your wisdom to come from my mouth.

Lamedh

89 Divine Mind, through you all of creation was manifested. 90 You made this world and surrounded it in love and faithfulness. 91 Your laws are the foundation for eternity, to be followed in service to you. 92 I study the workings of your laws and I am comforted. 93 Divine law fills me with gratitude and I affirm your presence. 94 I study your covenants and I am redeemed. 95 I have nothing and no one to fear when I consider all your precepts. 96 There is no limit to the Truth that can be found when I study your laws.

Mem

97 Divine law comes to me in my times of meditation. 98 Your wisdom stays with me and directs my thoughts and actions. 99 When in the presence of wise people I listen for your precepts. 100 My understanding is increased each time that I meditate on your laws. 101 My faith keeps me from straying into error thinking. 102 Your laws are my foundation for they come from you. 103 They bring me joy and comfort. 104 My spiritual understanding is increased; and I avoid wrongdoing because of it.

Nuh

105 Your words enlighten my mind and my actions. 106 I dedicate myself to your teachings and I will study them with great care. 107 Even in my distress I have gotten comfort from your words. 108 May my words of thanks be acceptable to you, God. 109 Through each day and night I will meditate on your wisdom. 110 I avoid error thoughts by studying your laws. 111 They give me strength of mind and spirit and they bring me joy. 112 I commit myself to the study of your words.

Samekh

113 I stay away from those who speak out against you, God, and I am faithful to your laws. 114 I find comfort in you at all times; I have faith in your words. 115 Material gains do not tempt me because of your teachings! 116 I will dedicate my life to your good works; my hope and faith remain in you. 117 Because of your wisdom I am lifted up; my consciousness of spiritual matters is increased. 118 I stay away from those who do not follow your laws; they have nothing to teach me. 119 Your laws give me strength against evildoers; I do not stray from them. 120 I speak of you with awe; I respect your precepts.

Ayin

121 I strive to live with amity and justice; with you I will not be oppressed. 122 I affirm your protection; I have nothing to fear. 123 I enter the silence with you and I find hope and redemption there. 124 I feel your love surrounding me and I want to learn more about you. 125 I wish to live my life in service to you, always honoring your words. 126 When I see evidence of wrongdoing, I pray for healing and for justice to be done. 127 Your laws mean more to me than pure gold, 128 and I am inspired to do good works in your name.

Pe

129 Your doctrine brings me joy; I will follow your teachings. 130 Through prayer and meditation I am enlightened; spiritual enrichment is mine. 131 I thirst for your words and I search for their meaning. 132 I believe in your love and mercy, and I know I am surrounded by them. 133 May I always follow your path; may I not stray into error thinking. 134 Show me the redemption that comes with spiritual consciousness. 135 Show me the light of your wisdom that I may follow it always. 136 I am saddened when I see injustice and oppression, for these go against your laws.

Tsadhe

137 You lead us to walk in right paths, and your teachings guide us. 138 When we follow your laws we are doing good works; others know that they can trust us to do good. 139 I am enlivened by your presence, even in the face of people who doubt you. 140 Your covenant with creation is eternal, and bound by love. 141 Though I am a small part of your creation I can do good deeds around me. 142 Your goodness is eternal, and your wisdom is Truth. 143 When I am afflicted I come to you for release from my trouble. 144 I will study your ways; may enlightenment be mine.

Qoph

145 I come to you in the silence, God, and I pray for your wisdom to come to me. 146 In my meditation I ask for your guidance; I will always follow your words. 147 Before the night is done I pray to you; my faith awaits an answer. 148 I do not sleep at night so that I may pray to you when the world is still. 149 I speak of my love for you; you, God, are all that I need. 150 For those who do not see you in themselves, I will pray that your goodness is made clear to them. 151 You are as close as my next breath, God, and I trust in your divine law completely. 152 You have fashioned creation according to your truth and wisdom, which are eternal.

Resh

153 In my distress I come to you for I can count on your love. 154 I ask for your protection; I ask that you be in me and around me. 155 For those who do not understand your ways I will pray that they are enlightened. 156 Your goodness and mercy are there for all who ask; I know that by asking, I will be protected.157 If any wish me ill, I will pray for them. 158 I will speak of your love to all who will listen. 159 I love to study your wisdom; my life is enriched because of it. 160 Your Truth is absolute; your words are eternal.

Sin and Shin

161 When I am troubled, I come to you for wisdom and guidance. 162 I trust that the right answer will come, as it always does. 163 I speak your truth, for false claims are against your teachings. 164 I give thanks and praise to you throughout my day, and into the night. 165 When I meditate, I find great peace within me and I am strengthened. 166 Your redemption comes from your overwhelming love. 167 I love your wisdom and your teachings. 168 I trust in your laws and I will follow them every day.

Taw

169 Today and every day I come to you God; I seek greater understanding of your word. 170 I come to you with humility; I ask that you be in me and around me. 171 My words will praise you and thank you, for your abundance is mine. 172 My songs will praise you and tell of your wisdom. 173 Extend your goodness to me, for I will follow your ways. 174 Your mercy and redemption are infinite.175 While I have breath I will praise you, and I will follow your laws. 176 You are my shepherd and you find me when I am troubled. I will always remember your laws.

Psalm 119 is the longest one in the Psalter. Its 176 verses lead to one overarching conclusion: That keeping God's commandments is the source of all right actions. I am to look to God for guidance when the path in front of me is obscured. If I do this with an open heart and a student's mind, God's wisdom will be revealed.

There is also a common thread of gratitude and humility running through these stanzas: the blessings of God's laws, coupled with the request for further insight in order to live a virtuous life. The writer expresses gratitude for the gifts that come with God's teachings. There is also a reason for gratitude that God's laws are immutable. The laws of creation do not waver, and even with our current scientific knowledge and advanced technology we have not yet cracked God's codes. The deeper our understanding becomes, the deeper the mystery.

PSALM 120

A song of ascents.

1 When I am troubled, I enter the silence and pray to God. 2 My thoughts are disturbed and I need guidance. 3 When I am confused, or distressed, I lose my way. 4 I am prone to thoughts that do not serve me. I ask for God's purifying fire to burn away my error thinking. 5 When I dwell on the desire for that which I do not need, I lose richness of spirit and my mind is unsettled. 6 Then I pray to God for release from sense consciousness. 7 I pray for the peace that Spirit brings so that I will know God's Truth.

The next 15 psalms all carry the superscription of "A song of ascents." What they have in common is an underlying belief that it is always right to commune with God and be open to God's love and wisdom.

Psalm 120 reminds me that I can always trust God. God is my refuge, never farther away than my willingness to reach out and surrender. God is freedom from thoughts that disrupt my forward motion. God and Spirit are the openers of all good doors and the guides to the next right thing to do.

PSALM 121

A song of ascents.

1 I lift up my prayers to God – how can I not be brought closer to God and Spirit? 2 All that I need comes from Divine Mind that made manifest the universe and our place in it. 3 The love of God embraces me – this love is eternal and there for all. 4 God lives in each of us and is our constant source of protection. 5 God's wisdom enlightens the spirit of any who seek it. 6 Either awake or asleep, there is comfort in God's everlasting goodness. 7 God's love protects us – it protects every living creature; 8 from our beginning to our last breath, God's love surrounds us.

This psalm reminds me that Divine Mind, God, existing without beginning or ending, is the energy from which the universe is expressed. Knowing that I am made of God's enduring light gives me great comfort. Psalm 121 is a psalm that reminds me to be courageous in the presence of God's love. With God, I find shelter. Knowing this helps me to live my best life without the crippling presence of fear to hold me back. It is that fear that keeps me stuck in a safe little rut.

My challenge comes in remembering this when times are hard. Faith tells me to believe that my creator gives me exactly what I need both in good times and in the middle of uncertainty. I have enough life history now that

I can look back and follow the threads that weave patterns of assurance that God's grace held me up when I needed it. If I need a keeper, which I absolutely do, God is my best choice.

PSALM 122

A song of ascents. Of David.

1 When I need respite, I joyfully go into the silence to find God and Spirit. 2 In my heart I know that here is where I will find the deepest peace of mind and soul. 3 I gather my thoughts and wait for serenity to settle upon me. 4 My mind is quieted and I give thanks to God for the guidance that will come. 5 I open myself to the flow of God's love. 6 My prayer is for all to know the depth of love coming to us from Divine Mind. 7 My hope is that peace will overcome distress. 8 My faith assures me that discord can be overcome with love. 9 I pray earnestly that all may experience God's abundant love and goodness.

Our electronic devices are designed to keep us updated on, well, everything we can imagine. "Breaking news" scrolls along the bottom of our TV's and pops up on our smart phones. The media bombard us with information, and advertisements, and the latest scandals. We live in a 24/7/365 world filled with politics and challenges and tragedies and, sometimes, a little good news.

Psalm 122 reminds me that there is always somewhere to go where I can find peace. Even if I enter the silence with turmoil of mind and heart, before long a blessed stillness settles in. With God's help I can arrange my jumbled thoughts into a coherent theme. I wait for God's wisdom to permeate my thoughts. Before long I feel a deep sense of assurance that God's love is the foundation upon which I can rest until an answer comes to me.

PSALM 123

A song of ascents.

1 When I elevate my thoughts beyond mere material consciousness, I find God. 2 I do not give in to thoughts of lack and discouragement; I am not enslaved by them. 3 I understand that God is the purest source of mercy, available to all who pray to overcome doubt and fear. 4 With God I find enduring grace, and I affirm its abundance.

I'd like to think that my soul is observant and open for business every day. Some days, though, I am more tuned in to those signs that God is at work. Other days I am not looking, or aware, until the moment has passed and I realize, in retrospect, that something holy has transpired. The earth doesn't tremble, fire doesn't issue forth, lightning bolts don't strike, it is only the knowledge that goodness and mercy prevailed, even if only for a few moments.

The superscription, "A Song of Ascents," implies that God can be found up in the heavens. Unity teaches me that I do not have to reach out to connect with God. God is within, as well as around, as close as a breath and a heartbeat. God is the source of ALL THAT IS, seen and unseen, personal and universal. I learn that God in me is my opportunity to manifest my best self, and I am acutely aware that accountability is an internal spiritual discipline.

PSALM 124

A song of ascents. Of David.

1 If I had not known God – in body, mind, and soul – 2 if I had not known God when distress found me, 3 I would have stayed in the deepest darkness I have ever known; 4 despair would have consumed me, dread would have been my only companion; 5 I would have been forever lost in my sorrow. 6 I praise God within me, and Spirit, who held me in love when I was adrift. 7 My prayers to God bound me together when it seemed that I was torn beyond repair. 8 God is my source of hope and faith, the God who created us all.

Psalm 124 reminds me of how often I have been in between life's trajectories and God's grace. Once a cascade of events has been set in motion, who decides where the pieces will land? Unimaginable forces of nature are unleashed when circumstances of weather combine to create what we call a "perfect storm," or a "super storm." The same phenomenon of chaos can catch us unaware as we go through our day-to-day lives.

When the change leads to a good outcome, we celebrate. When we are knocked off our foundation by an unanticipated turn of events, it can feel as though there is nothing of substance to hold us together. At times like these, it is a great comfort to me to use Unity principles, most especially the understanding that God is inextricably bound into the very cells of my being.

In *The Revealing Word*, Charles Fillmore writes this: "God immanent – This refers to the all-pervading and indwelling presence of God, the life and intelligence permeating the universe. Jesus lovingly revealed that the

Father is within man, forever resident in the invisible side of man's nature. Paul also set forth this truth when he wrote of 'one God and Father of all, who is over all, and through all, and in all' (Eph. 4:6)." [50]

PSALM 125

A song of ascents.

1 I place my faith in God from whom love emanates, and it endures for all eternity. 2 My thoughts are exalted when I commune with God and I know a perfect peace. 3 I will not be swayed from my belief in God's wisdom and goodness, and I will resist false claims. 4 Knowing that God's goodness is always available, I am able to withstand any challenge. 5 Those who rely on error thinking will struggle on their path. I will pray for them to know peace.

Unity teaches me about the power of choice, and how a choice can manifest goodness or iniquity. Psalm 125 reminds me that even those who are virtuous are free to choose from the wide range of human behaviors and thoughts. Through Unity, I know that love and Christ consciousness are within me, able to be accessed with prayer and meditation. Or, I can choose to live in sense consciousness and make decisions governed by an unruly ego. One way strengthens faith. One way makes faith vulnerable to a kind of silent erosion.

Faith is a gift from God. It is also the means through which I know God. Faith is a source of wisdom and a path to compassion. Faith is the power that comes with absolute trust in God. No matter the time and date, no

---

50   Fillmore, Charles, *The Revealing Word*, 85-86.

matter the circumstance, no matter if it is peril or celebration, God is present. God may speak differently to each of us, but the message is rooted in grace.

PSALM 126

A song of ascents.

1 If we are lost, God will raise us up and guide us. 2 Our spirits will know happiness, our hearts will be filled with joy. Those around us will see us as children of God. 3 There is no end to God's goodness, and we will always benefit from it. 4 There is no lack of God's abundance, it is like finding water in the driest places. 5 Even in our sorrow we are lifted up by God's love. 6 When we mourn, yet carry faith in our hearts, we will be lifted up by God's love.

I am paraphrasing a saying I once kept on the refrigerator: THE WILL OF GOD WILL NEVER TAKE YOU WHERE THE GRACE OF GOD CANNOT PROTECT YOU. Believing this gives me such a sense of safety and security, even in the midst of difficulties. I know that God's love and goodness will shore up my faith when I am shaken. Psalm 126 tells me that wherever I am, God is within me and around me. That's all the assurance that I need.

PSALM 127

A song of ascents. Of Solomon.

1 Without the sure knowledge of God's love, my foundation can be shaken. When I do not seek God's wisdom, my way is not clear. 2 If I am mired in false claims and error thinking,

I am not secure – for I have forgotten that God provides me
with all that I need. 3 My meditations bring me to a place of
gladness, and I am blessed. 4 Prayers give wings to the words
that I send to God. 5 God will bless me with guidance and
wise answers.

Solomon is known for his wisdom. The sentiment in the opening lines that things work better with God's imprimatur, makes absolute sense to me. Any endeavor of mine is better served when I am mindful of God's enduring grace. After all, if a butterfly's fluttering wings contribute to a windstorm half a world away, how powerful is an action rooted in God's love and performed with kindness? This psalm is a reminder to me that it is best to match my outward behaviors with an inner sense of reverence for all of God's creation.

PSALM 128

A song of ascents.

1 Praise God as the source of all blessings, praise God for the
wisdom found through God. 2 God's creation is an infinite
source of abundance; it is there for everyone. 3 Those who love
God know that faith is a powerful force, and that faith lived
out brings joy to a home. 4 All who approach God with rever-
ence and praise will know God's peace. 5 God is within each
one, bringing thoughts of good; prayers to God bring peace
and understanding every day. 6 Thoughts based in God's com-
passion lead to a life of good works.

Psalm 128 reminds me of the spiritual discipline required to revere God and to follow God's ways. This calls for a purity of intention that can't be set aside when it suits me to do so, and this is where I invariably make my journey more complicated than it needs to be. When I don't listen to that "still, small voice" is when I lose touch with God's Truth.

Entering into communion with God brings a spiritual richness: a sense of absolute belonging to the flow of God's creative wellspring. This is not belonging in the sense of being entitled, or better than. This is belonging as in being an essential thread in the tapestry of life, intertwined with the pattern in ways that support its shapes and colors; belonging as in the assurance that a joy-filled life is made up of purposeful work, nourishment of body and soul, kindness at all times, and an absolute trust that all is as it should be.

PSALM 129

A song of ascents.

1 "I have come to know distress in my life," I say; 2 "I have carried a burden since my youth, but I have done it with the strength of God in me. 3 I have been hurt in many ways. 4 With God's help, I have known spiritual freedom from these bonds. 5 When I meditate with God, my thoughts are uplifted and I know peace. 6 My sorrows fade away like morning dew. 7 I do not fill my thoughts with the stain of anguish. 8 Instead I find the blessings of God's love that are within me and all around me."

There is a saying: EVERYONE IS FIGHTING A BATTLE YOU KNOW NOTHING ABOUT. BE KIND. Psalm 129 reminds me that we all carry wounds from experiences of cruelty, or betrayal, or abandonment, or our own misguided behavior.

One of the most important lessons that I have gotten from Unity teachings is that I have the ability to deny the power of wounded-ness and to affirm that with God's love and goodness I can reframe my thinking. I can change my entire perspective from a victim mentality to an awareness that I am strong and capable of overcoming.

In Myrtle Fillmore's book, *How To Let God Help You*, she writes: "Do not bother about anything that has been, or that seems to be taking place at present, or that is to come in the future. Leave past, present, and future in God's hands. Leave yourself in God's care and keeping, and just do that which will furnish Spirit with the necessary materials to be converted into harmony of soul, strength and health of body. Keep your thoughts free from worry. Keep them on matters close at hand, on God's presence and power."[51]

PSALM 130

A song of ascents.

1 When I am deeply troubled, I reach out to you, God. 2 I enter the silence with you and my prayers take form. 3 You do not count my iniquities, but leave them for me to consider. 4 I know the depth of your love and forgiveness, and I find comfort in that knowledge. 5 When I meditate, both God and Spirit

---

51 Fillmore, Myrtle, *How To Let God Help You*, 19.

are manifested to me, and I trust in their love. 6 I learn from God when I pray, and I wait for God's wisdom to come into my awareness. 7 I know that I can place my hopes into God's care, for God is the source of love and goodness. 8 With God, redemption is always possible.

God does not count our iniquities. That is the promise of Psalm 130. Forgiveness comes from God, as do love and grace. I must never take these promises for granted, nor may I assume that I am entitled to receive them freely. I don't think that God withholds mercy or redemption. I am the one who forgets to do my part of living in a way that seeks the next right action, thought, or deed. This means that I examine my actions through the lens of personal responsibility and that I am not afraid to say so if my behavior is out of line. It means that I understand the cause and effect of my conduct, and that I accept the consequences.

I used to think I was entirely self-sufficient, that I could fully rely on myself to navigate my life. It has taken me years to realize the arrogance of this kind of pride. I have been brought down enough times, and have subsequently been lifted back up by the grace of God. That is the grace that has opened my eyes to the blessings of help that comes from so many sources.

PSALM 131

A song of ascents. Of David.

1 God, I pray for the spirit of humility to dwell within me; I want only to be grateful for the abundance that you make manifest for all. 2 When I am in your presence I am as peaceful

as a sleeping child; like a sleeping child I find peace. 3 I place
my trust in you, God, today and every day.

Several years ago I read *The Story of Unity*, a book given to me when I
joined Unity of Naples. I was hungry to learn about the origins of this spiritual movement. Throughout the book are examples of the humble beginnings of Unity, shepherded by the Fillmore's. They did not seek wealth or
fame, but they were relentless advocates for the riches that lie inside each
of us. They did not seek God in prestigious circles or magnificent temples.
Instead they wrote and spoke about finding God in the silence that underlies all of creation, in the silence within each of us. They based their work
on Jesus' teachings; Jesus, who exhorts us to find the kingdom within.

Psalm 131 speaks of the kind of peace and comfort that cannot be shaken,
because it comes from the deepest part of us. Once that peace is experienced, there is no going back. There may be times when the connection
fades or is frayed by difficult circumstances, but it does not break. The
source of inner peace comes from a deep trust that God is, just that, God IS.

PSALM 132

A song of ascents.

1 God's love knows no boundaries. 2 In turn, those who love
God make a sacred vow to uphold this divine gift. 3 They will
not rest, 4 they do not sleep, 5 until they have given thanks and
opened their hearts to receive this precious energy. 6 There is
no end to the substance of love, it is found throughout creation.
7 It is in the temple and in the highest and lowest places. 8
Love is carried by the whisper of Spirit, and in the divine fire

that exists in each living thing. 9 The wisest among us know of God's love and are filled with joy. 10 Harmony and love are found among those whose center is a grateful heart. 11 God has a covenant with creation: love will keep the stars in their places for eternity. 12 Those who honor the passion that God holds for creation live with gladness. 13 The human family is united by God's love, given freely to all. 14 Love upholds us and is the source of all good health. 15 Love is abundant goodness. 16 It is not denied to any, both the wise and the foolish are its recipients. 17 Love brings a lightness of being and causes good things to appear. 18 Those who pray for enlightenment will feel the love of God.

Psalm 132, in its original form, is about King David setting out to build a temple where God could dwell. Unity teaches me that God's dwelling place is in us, among us, and all around creation. As a person of faith I believe that God's love is manifested throughout ALL THAT IS, and that God's main temple is out in the everyday world. While we honor God when we build elaborate places of worship, they are not the only places in which to witness God's love and grace. Jesus knew that when he went to the temple and saw it had become a secular place of business. We should all remember what he did next.

So much of faith is anchored by symbols and symbolic acts. One morning, having been outside to see Venus shining hugely over the mountains, I realized that this pure vision of God's accomplishments is critical to the foundation of my beliefs. The challenge for my truest faith is to strike a balance between loving the buildings and rituals of my church, and following the call to see God through unobstructed eyes.

Psalm 132 is also about God's love for all creation. In The Revealing Word there is a definition for LOVE: "The pure essence of being that binds together the whole human family. Of all the attributes of God, love is undoubtedly the most beautiful. In Divine Mind, love is the power that joins and binds in divine harmony the universe and everything in it; the great harmonizing principle known to man. Divine love is impersonal; it loves for the sake of loving. It is not concerned with what or who it loves, nor with a return of love. Like the sun, its joy is in the shining forth of its nature."[52]

PSALM 133

A song of ascents. Of David.

1 When people acknowledge precious Spirit that dwells within, we shall all be one with God. 2 There will be one universal prayer whose words tell of unity with God. 3 All thoughts will join together in one great hymn to God, and we will all be blessed.

I wonder why it is that when people are grouped together we behave like chickens, and establish a pecking order. Some are considered more exalted than others. This creates a system of false beliefs, a kind of caste system where someone has to be the lowly Untouchable while another lives as a proud Brahman, a member of the highest class among Hindus.

So many tragedies could be averted if interconnection was the creed that humans adopted as a foundation to build upon. But that is not the way that we choose to live, and the evidence is all around us. From the time

---

52   Fillmore, Charles, *The Revealing Word*, 124-125.

that hominids discovered that hunting tools were also weapons to be used against another, union was called into question. And so it continues to this day.

Psalm 133 is a poignant one, describing a utopian time. But it reminds me that I can believe in the preciousness of another person. I know that God's grace carries with it opportunities to make connections with the energies of other souls. Each bond is precious, and there is no other like it. This is my lesson for learning about what really matters in my life.

PSALM 134

A song of ascents.

1 Give thanks to God for those who do not sleep when it is dark, but who give their gifts to those who need them. 2 Pray for them and thank God for their labors. 3 God, who is our creator, surrounds them with love to carry them through the night.

This is the last of the songs of ascent.

Psalm 134 has always resonated with me. As a nurse for over four decades I worked my share of night shifts, but my most vivid memories are of working in hospice and being on call at night. During the fifteen years that I worked in hospice, I can't count the number of times when the phone rang and I drove through the night air to reach a home, not knowing exactly what I would find when I entered.

In the beginning, my own fears and inexperience were what I had to set aside as I entered the house. Before long, though, I knew what I was supposed to do, but each family had different dynamics, so I quickly had to learn what I was *expected* to do in each case. Walking into a home where someone has just died, or is actively dying, or is having some sort of crisis, I learned to quiet myself with my mantra: "May the words of my mouth and the meditations of my heart be acceptable in your sight, O God." (Psalm 19)

Hospice work is a calling. Hospice work, in the deepest and darkest part of the night, is an opportunity to encounter God in the midst of raw sorrow. Something about a mission in the silence of the night made it seem holy to me, and so, despite, or because of, my own discomfort and exhaustion, God rode with me on this ministry.

PSALM 135

1 Give thanks to God. Let words of praise come from your mouth, words that honor God, 2 all of you who work for justice and peace in this world. 3 Give praise to God wherever you may be; sing songs of redemption and love. 4 For God lives within us all, and we are all God's children. 5 God's powers extend to each of us and to the farthest regions of the universe. 6 God's love manifests as stars and planets and the creatures than inhabit them. 7 Divine laws order the clouds and the wind and rain; the power of lightning belongs to God. 8 God is also gently in the midst of all sorrows. 9 God leads us through the clamor of material consciousness as we open our hearts to Spirit. 10 God's protection is ours without asking. 11 God leads us beyond thoughts of physical and material gain and lifts us to the realm of Spirit – 12 God's wisdom is ours when we pray for it. 13 When we speak God's name and seek God's words we are strengthened. 14 For God is our source of mercy and love. 15 There are some who follow false claims, without regard for God's love and wisdom. 16 They speak only of material gains, and they do not see the glory in God's creation. 17 They do not want the guidance of Spirit, nor do they use their senses to explore God's living world. 18 They are rooted in material consciousness and they do not speak of spiritual enlightenment. 19 But God leads us to a greater knowledge of matters of spirit, to a new consciousness. 20 God's love deserves our praise and gratitude for its gifts. 21 Praise God, and all those who live with God's love and peace in their hearts.

Psalm 135 echoes a few verses from Psalm 115, particularly about thinking beyond the material world to the realm of Spirit. The lesson that I get from both poems is to remember what is really important and life-giving to me. Treasures and possessions are tangible and gratifying, adding a sense of security to my life. They are visible proof of my "success" and "hard work." But I also know that possessions can weigh me down.

I once gave a seminar about how change can teach us what is truly essential to us. I asked the participants to think about this: assuming that people and animals are safe, what would you take with you if your house was burning to the ground?

Like so many of the women in the seminar, I would take my pictures. Squares of black and white, rectangles with colors, paper memories of the people and places that are precious to me. Small reminders of who I have been and where I have come from, things with no intrinsic value to anyone but me. They are my memory keepers, images that remind me of the many blessings given to me through the mercy and compassion of my Creator.

PSALM 136

1 Praise God and give thanks for God's goodness. God loves us all. 2 God almighty lives within us. God loves us all. 3 There is but one God. God loves us all. 4 God's substance manifests as life. God loves us all. 5 God's universe is infinite. God loves us all. 6 The earth and the sea are made by God. God loves us all. 7 From fire light to star light, God is there. God loves us all. 8 The sun by day, 9 and the moon by night are God's. God loves us all. 10 In the midst of tragedy God appears. God loves us all. 11 God offers us spiritual enlightenment. God loves us all. 12 God's strength knows no limits. God loves us all. 13 God is the maker of miracles. God loves us all. 14 God's protection is assured. God loves us all. 15 With prayer, we know God's works. God loves us all. 16 When we are lost, God is a beacon. God loves us all. 17 When we are caught in material consciousness, God offers Spirit to us. God loves us all. 18 When false claims lead us on, God's wisdom will prevail when we meditate. God loves us all. 19 If we are rooted in sense consciousness, God's truth teaches us another way. God loves us all. 20 God directs our senses to look beyond what we can see. God loves us all. 21 God's gifts are there for all who want them. God loves us all. 22 We are given what we need through God's abundance. God loves us all. 23 When we are deeply troubled, God is a constant companion. God loves us all. 24 We are set free through God's abiding love. God loves us all. 25 When we are hungry in spirit, God provides food. God loves us all. 26 Praise God and give thanks for God's abiding presence. God loves us all.

Psalm 136 starts with praise and thanks, and ends with love. The refrain at the end of each verse says that God's love leaves no one out, that God loves us all. It is marvelous to me to consider the juxtaposition of the power that creates the universe and the gentleness of a love that never goes away. Where these two intersect is where I can point to the primal proof of Creator and Creation.

A wise young pastor asked my congregation, "Where did you see God this week?" We were to turn to our neighbor for answers, given and received. Some shared their answers: in nature, in family and friends, at work, in the Emergency Room, in the middle of a crisis. No one had seen God on a throne, pitching lightning bolts toward earth. It seems that God is glimpsed in the minutiae of day-to-day living. To me, that is the definition of hope, that in my ordinary hours I can trust that God will appear some-where in the details, if I am paying attention.

This psalm tells me that in addition to God's omnipresence, I am assured that God loves ALL of us. I am told that God's love for creation is stead-fast. Not only did God manifest ALL THAT IS, God is the caretaker of ALL THAT IS. Out of this nurture, freely given, the roots of gratitude are firmly planted for God's unconditional love. God loves us all.

PSALM 137

1 In my sorrow, as I weep, my thoughts are confused and in disarray. 2 The music is gone from my soul, 3 I cannot find my song even though I am told that singing leads to joy. 4 I am in an unfamiliar place, how can I sing when I am lost? 5 I have forgotten that my soul can know peace. 6 My mouth is filled with ashes and my words are bound together in my throat. 7

I come to God an empty vessel, longing to be filled with living water. 8 I pray for relief from my distress and I am reminded that God is with me through any adversity. 9 I reach out to God, and my song is gently and carefully restored.

Psalm 137 is one of the most poignant poems in the Psalter. It calls forth the echoes of the losses that are an inevitable part of life. At some point, sorrow visits everyone: bright and hot at first, it eventually fades into a shadow life of its own. When sorrow is new, its companion is the weeping that wracks body and soul. When sorrow has been woven into the fabric of a life it can strengthen us, or it can ruin us.

During the first Iraq war, my son was six. Television news was filled with images of oil wells burning, and predictions of a dire oil shortage as a result. One night after he was tucked in bed he told me that he was worried for all of the people who would be cold because they would not have oil for heat during the winter. Then, from a tender heart, came this question: "Why is it I feel sadness all the way to the bottom of my heart and most people only feel it at the top of theirs?"

That is a question that deserves an answer right on the spot, and "I don't know" was not it. Only God helped me to find the words, kneeling by his bed in the dark. This is what came to me. I told him he had been given a gift to be able to feel life deeply and with compassion. I also told him that with this ability he would have to face sorrows with great courage and, sometimes, with great pain. As young as he was, he told me he understood what I was saying.

When sorrow makes its appearance the best that I know to do is to go to the deepest part of me, where God and I dwell together. When I find my way to that safe and sacred place, when I remember what it takes to get there, I will be in God's hands.

PSALM 138

Of David.

1 I send my thanks and praise for the many manifestations of God in creation. 2 God lives in me, and I find God all around me. God is in everything that my senses take in, and God's promise of abundance never ends. 3 When I enter the silence to commune with God, my spirit is strengthened. 4 Body, mind, and soul are filled with gratitude for all of God's gifts. 5 God puts a song in my heart, a song of praise and thanksgiving. 6 There is no end to God's love; all creatures receive it. 7 When I am in distress, I pray to you and I am released. You lift me up in the midst of trouble so that I can overcome it. 8 Your wisdom, love and goodness create life in your image – you do not leave us unprepared.

Our Creator has endowed me with free will, which to me means that I am on my own to make choices about every aspect of my life. God has also put in place the natural order of creation: of birth and death, of order and chaos, and the stunningly complex formulas that underlie it all. As a citizen of the cosmos I have opportunities, but I also have obligations to make choices that resonate with my belief in God's elegant systems.

I come prepared for this life because of the gifts that God has placed in me and around me. I am safe by virtue of the grace that God has extended my way: a brain with which to contemplate, a heart with which to feel joy and sorrow, a soul that is half mine and half God's, and a relatively healthy body with which to carry these important parts.

In *The Revealing Word*, Charles Fillmore writes this about our make-up: "Man is spirit, soul, and body. Spirit is the I AM, the individuality. The body is soul expressing, and soul includes the conscious and subconscious minds. Soul makes the body, the body is the outer expression of the soul, and bodily health is in exact correspondence to the health of the soul."[53]

PSALM 139

For the director of music. Of David. A psalm.

1 God, you have made me in your image, and you dwell within me. 2 You know my thoughts and my actions because we are inextricably one. 3 I bring my thoughts and prayers to you; you know of them before I do. 4 If I speak, you hear me before the words leave my mouth. 5 You are within me and around me and I feel your presence. 6 If I try to understand the vastness of your works, my mind cannot grasp it all. 7 Wherever I am, you and Spirit are there. Why would I want to escape your presence? 8 The realm of your Divine Mind surrounds me; if I am laid low I seek your wisdom. 9 Even if I could fly like a bird to places unknown you are with me. 10 Your firm guidance is as close as my next prayer. 11 When I am caught in sense consciousness, your love lights my way to you, 12 and when I forget to listen, your counsel somehow comes to me. 13 God, you were there at my beginning; your divine presence imbued my cells with life and I was made. 14 I give thanks and

---

53   Fillmore, Charles, *The Revealing Word*, 182.

praise for your gift; your very breath of life. 15 Each day in my mother's womb brought a miraculous change, and I developed according to your plan. 16 You knew me before anyone else and you have been with me since. 17 I meditate on your vast wisdom. Your knowledge encompasses the universe. 18 Divine Mind conceived the universe, then brought it into being with divine order. 19 Your goodness is all around us. It is there for everyone to partake, even those who do not know of you. 20 I will always praise your name, even in the company of those who do not know of you. 21 I will speak of your goodness and love, and pray that understanding comes with my words. 22 If there is someone who doubts you, I will speak kindly to them of your love. 23 Live in my heart, God, so that I may manifest your goodness and demonstrate your peace. 24 Lead me away from selfish behavior so that I may devote my life to you.

This is the psalm that brings comfort to me faster than any other. I think of it as a declaration of the deepest intimacy of all, and of the purest form of love with which God surrounds me. In Psalm 139 I feel assured that God knows me inside and out, flaws and all, and that there is no room in this relationship for shame or fear. In these verses I am given the opportunity to fully realize that God is both deeply personal and profoundly cosmic, and that I am an integral part of God's ALL THAT IS.

My relationship with God is the most intimate one that I will ever have. Being able to completely trust that God is the absolute source of love and grace, that God has no hidden agenda, and that I am a beloved child of God, means I can be in this relationship with complete trust and confidence.

Unity teaches me to seek the God particle within me, my personal Higgs Boson that has been a part of me in this life and beyond. Every living being carries a spark of God at its core. This is what ultimately unites us as living creations loved into being by Divine Mind.

PSALM 140

For the director of music. A psalm of David.

1 God, I find myself in an uncomfortable place; I am surrounded by those whose words uphold untruths, 2 whose thoughts are of subversion. 3 With your help I will deny their devious ways; I will not take part in their betrayal. 4 I will affirm your protection from people who do not think as I do, who have devised clever ways to avoid the truth. 5 I will affirm your truth and I will not participate in any deceitful plans. 6 I enter the silence to meditate on ways of integrity and I wait for your guidance. 7 You are my foundation and my source of wisdom. 8 Those who delight in error thoughts are not honest in their dealings with others. 9 When I am with them their words are not sincere or straightforward. 10 I pray for knowledge of my next actions so that I will not be mired in their iniquities. 11 Those who dishonor others should be called to account; I pray that I will remove myself from their midst. 12 When I consider your wisdom I know that you uphold justice at all times. 13 I pray that I may discern ways that promote equity for all.

For the last few years of my nursing career I was a nurse in a middle school. In the microcosm that was my school, the kind of drama portrayed in Psalm 140 played itself out on a daily basis. There were a handful of students who thrived on creating a maelstrom that they could watch unfold from the sidelines. Causing disruption and pain was their modus operandi and, as young as they were, there were already pretty good at what they did.

If this sounds harsh, I would invite you into my little nursing office where the victims of these kinds of power plays came to seek some peace and support. I can remember anger rising in me which on most days I could temper and remember to pray for both the victim and the perpetrator.

In one of the afterschool programs that I co-led, we worked with a group of students who were particularly interested in learning ways of helping students who were the victims of bullying – either in person or in cyberspace. One of our meetings involved the kids watching the movie, "Bully." It is a powerful film about the violence that children are capable of perpetrating on another child. It paints an ugly picture of the scarcity of helpful responses from adults, who often waved off bullying as "kids will be kids."

In the film, the kids enduring the bullying were simply trying to find a way through childhood and adolescence by going to school, having friends, taking part in activities of interest to them. But, wherever the bullies lurked, these childhood tasks were rendered difficult if not impossible. The subsequent despair of two of the children featured in the film led them to commit suicide. That such sadness can permeate a young child is heartbreaking. Yet it happens every day in all communities in our country. These are times and circumstances that require us to stand up for kindness.

PSALM 141

A psalm of David.

1 At this moment, God, I enter the silence with you. 2 I wait quietly for my prayer to take form and join with you; my heart is open and ready to receive your wisdom. 3 May the words of my prayer reflect the gratitude that I feel towards you. 4 I am drawn to your peace and your love; I pray that I may practice these in my daily life. 4 I am ready for any lessons that come from this prayer – may I be centered in kindness as I receive them. 5 I pray for right relations with those whom I encounter today. I am willing to go forth with a peaceful heart and mind. 6 When I come across false claims I pray for the willingness to seek your Truth. 7 In this way is error thinking deflected and my path to you is made clear. 8 I pray that I may see the effects of precious Spirit at work throughout the day. 9 I rely on your wisdom to guide me at all times. 10 I pray that I may manifest your goodness today and every day.

I have been told that there are many ways to pray. Psalm 141 reminds me of the power of a thoughtful prayer, composed in the silence, in the presence of God. So many times my prayer is made on the fly, literally thrown out into the ether without a lot of thought behind it. That is usually a foolish or selfish prayer that expects immediate action and is soon forgotten. It can be as mundane as praying for a break in the traffic so I won't be late to wherever I am supposed to be.

I used to stand next to a gentleman in church who, during a prayer, would hold his hands out, palms up. While the rest of us would bow our heads and keep our hands closed and down, he would strike the pose of give and take. His hands were open so that the energy of the prayer could more freely move in and out of him; so that the essence of precious Spirit might enter and feel the depth of his faith; so that if God had a need for anything from him there would be no barrier. I know this because I asked him about his prayer practice one day after church.

As a child, I was taught that bedtime prayer that started out with the words, "Now I lay me down to sleep, I pray the Lord my soul to keep." The rest of the words were terrifying . "If I die before I wake, I pray the Lord my soul to take." I vowed never to teach my children those words. And, I never did.

Thankfully, Unity teaches me to take my prayers to God in language that is mine alone. My prayer can be as gentle and loving as it needs to be. Even when I am distressed, my prayer can be fashioned out of words of comfort. It is my communion with God and with Spirit.

PSALM 142

A maskil of David. When he was in the cave. A prayer.

1 Out of my distress I call to you, God; I ask that your mercy wash over me. 2 I have prayed and meditated and opened myself to your wisdom and your truth. 3 I feel your presence ever near me, even in my weakest moments. You are with me as I live out each day. 4 When I enter the silence with you I am never alone. Your loving presence is my companion. 5 When I form the words of my prayers, I start with gratitude for your goodness that is always with me. 6 If I am in need, I give thanks for your abundance; I find my way through the temptations of material things. 7 I am free from such dependence because I trust that I have just what I need. Others can see that

I am prosperous in matters of spirit because of you, God.

Psalm 142 is a prayer from someone with a need for mercy and support. When I think about what it feels like when my spirit is faint, I know distress. I can enter into a cloud of doubt that my weaknesses will ever turn to strengths. This leads to fear that my psyche has cracks that can't be repaired, which in turn leads to a tired longing to be happy and whole again. It is a battle between the optimism I crave and the discouragement I loathe. Do I call out for God's peace, or do I try to find it elsewhere? That is a challenge that I face in my weakest moments.

I know without a doubt God speaks the language of sorrow, and God hears the voices of fear and hurt. When I can't think clearly about something in my life is when I need to pray and meditate, and trust that I will get understanding and guidance. When my vision only reveals a one-way street, it makes perfect sense that in careful prayer and discernment I will find more than one way to proceed.

Psalm 142 is a reminder of the power that lies with putting my thoughts into a coherent pattern that I can offer up in prayer. The details of my life are my own responsibility, and organizing them into an offering to my Creator is the gift I can give God. The freedom to do this is God's gift to me.

PSALM 143

A psalm of David.

1 God, I am in need of your wisdom and protection; I know that your love and comfort are mine when I most need them.

2 I consider my prayer carefully, so that I may come to you humbly, as your servant. 3 Some days I struggle with my errant thoughts and I am lost in them; my spirit is in darkness. 4 My confidence is shaken and my heart is empty. 5 I find a quiet place from which to consider all of your power; I think of the vastness of your creation. 6 I lift my hands in prayer, longing to drink from your living waters. 7 If I am fearful, I remember that you are always with me. 8 When a long night turns into daylight I know that my meditation has carried me along, and that I have a direction in which to go. 9 I affirm the power of prayers carried to you and to Spirit. 10 I learn what I can do to live according to your goodness and mercy. 11 I speak your name in my soul, knowing that you are there in the silence. 12 When I pray to you and ask to do your will, I know that I will be led in right ways.

Psalm 143 is a statement of what is possible when I start my day with reflection and with an open mind and heart. I know that each psalm is a harbinger of sorts, an opening to God's wisdom that can carry me through the day. It doesn't really matter that these prayer/poems were written so very long ago, or that they have been subject to hundreds of revisions, interpretations and translations. The essential message is intact: GOD IS, and so am I.

I ask that my morning meditations stay with me throughout the day so that I will remember to use my time wisely. Let me be on the lookout for God moments that bring lessons, or reassurance, or guidance, or comfort. Let me remember to breathe, to breathe in hope and confidence, and breathe out doubt and worry. Breathe and place one foot carefully in front of the other, walking in gratitude. Listen to my mind and soul, both of whom are happier when I remember the power of grace in my life. Keep my thoughts based in faith that the works of God's hands have enriched my life, over and over again.

PSALM 144

Of David.

1 I give thanks and praise to God, in whom I have my being, whose love encompasses me. 2 Love is the power with which God's creation is made; God's love secures my place in this creation. 3 God has given humans the power of thought, the gift of words, the ability to care for others. 4 No matter the length of someone's days, their life is precious in God's sight. 5 God's laws of nature make mountains smoke and send forth fire. 6 Power strikes the earth as lightning flares above us. 7 This same power watches over me and I am protected, 8 defended from any distress that comes to me. 9 I will sing songs of praise and thanks, and I will be open to receive Spirit, 10 who brings the whisper of God's love. I am surrounded 11 by God's infinite capacity for goodness, and I know God's Truth. 12 All creatures live according to God's divine law that manifests divine love. 13 We are surrounded by God's abundance to meet any need. Prosperity exists for all to envision, each in their own way. 14 We are given the means to overcome burdens and each can affirm God's goodness. Pain and sorrow can be subdued with prayer and meditation. 15 God's blessings exist for all people; we are all children of God.

A friend of mine recently lost her mother. Her grief is palpable. We agreed that when a mother dies, we feel like orphans who will never again be loved in quite the same way. For me there was a time after my mother left this earth when I could not even be comforted by the love of God. I was 32 years old, and pregnant with my daughter. I pained me beyond words that my mother would not get to know her first grandchild. I went for long walks and talked to God about my loss, which felt impenetrable.

One day I found a book in the house that I had never seen before. The title escapes me now, but in it was a quotation by the philosopher and mystic, Teilhard de Chardin. The book has since disappeared, so I have to paraphrase. Chardin wrote about our search for God, and the difficulties that can accompany this quest when we are in great distress. He wrote that God, like a mother, comes to gently hold us and our anguish. I remember clearly that those words gave me a deep sense of being cared for. That was the first moment of comfort I experienced after my mother's transition.

The older I get, and the closer I get to my own transition, the more I appreciate the beginning of each new day. Every morning brings a promise of a day of endless possibilities. How will I use this day? Will I behave in ways that honor my creator? Will I contribute something of value, something that adds to the smoothness of morning passing into night? Will I acknowledge, through my words and my actions, that God's love is the most precious gift of all? Will I be on the lookout for the God moments in my day?

PSALM 145

A psalm of praise. Of David.

1 I lift up my spirit to you, my God; I speak of you with words of praise and thanksgiving. 2 You are with me every day, and for that I am filled with gratitude. 3 You are the Divine Absolute; no one can completely understand your infinite creation. 4 You are with us always; even those to come will know of your presence. 5 Evidence of your glorious creation is all around us – in my meditations I acknowledge your grandeur. 6 The power of the universe is seen in the budding of a flower – I am in awe when I witness such proof. 7 Each one can reach for your abundance and tell others about it. 8 Your grace and compassion are manifested wherever love abides. 9 Your goodness is demonstrated throughout creation by your love of each creature in it. 10 Those who know of you praise you; your faithful people love you in turn. 11 Each one tells a story of their relationship with you, 12 so that others may learn of your love and abundance. 13 There is no end to you, and you hold all of your creation in steadfast love. 14 When I falter, I pray to you for guidance and support. You lift me up. 15 I am given all that I need because of your wisdom and love. 16 Your goodness is available to all. 17 You lead us in right ways and our faith sustains us. 18 You are as close as my next breath, and I pray to know your Truth. 19 Those who hold you in awe know you best; you are woven into their prayers. 20 Your wisdom is there to be studied, to teach us to avoid false claims and error thinking. 21 I will always praise you, God. Let us each praise you in our own way.

Number 145 is the last psalm attributed to David, and it come from a place of joy and praise. Through the triumphs and regrets in life, God is the constant from everlasting to everlasting!

The original versions of all the psalms write about a God who is "out there" somewhere. They praise God's greatness, God's goodness, God's mercy, God's sovereignty, and God's care that exists at a distance that only some can reach. We are invited to address God from afar.

Unity teachings tell me otherwise. I am to look within for the Christ nature, that proof of God's love for me. I am to look within to find God. This way of thinking requires a different kind of courage and a new way of perceiving the presence of God. It takes a certain boldness of spirit to truly believe there is a powerful God spark shining in my soul.

Unity invites me to enter into the holy silence in order to quiet the chattering of doubt and fear. This becomes a silence where I can affirm the power and presence of God and Spirit. I think of the line from an old hymn: "Breathe on me, breath of God." To that comforting phrase I add, "Breathe *in* me, breath of God. Breathe *with* me, breath of God."

PSALM 146

1 I praise God. My soul pays homage to God. 2 I will always sing songs of acclamation to God; for as long as I live I will praise God. 3 I do not put my trust only in material things, for they do not enrich my soul. 4 When I depart this earth, they do not come with me. 5 But the blessings of God carry my hopes safely through my days and nights. 6 God is the creator of All That Is – the visible and the invisible are God's. 7 In my meditations I learn that God loves good works that lift up the oppressed and feed the hungry. God offers freedom of thought to those who seek it. 8 God gives spiritual enlightenment to those who are searching, so that their spirit may be lifted up. 9 God welcomes the stranger, and loves those who are alone. 10 God is the Absolute, the source of everything forever and ever. Praise God.

God is a patient teacher, delivering a message of love and goodness to each generation, relying on us to demonstrate care and compassion. I am a reluctant pupil sometimes, forgetting what my true mission is about. In my opinion, it is sometimes hard work to love everyone, and I am unsuccessful more times than I care to admit.

One morning at my middle school, I was walking in one of the 7th grade halls where there were exhibits of a writing exercise about a utopian world. Some students filled an entire page, some had only a few sentences, some had drawings mixed in with their words. Since I was not in a hurry, I decided to stop and take in a few of their papers. I thought I might find some that saw utopia as a place for frequent trips to the mall, or an unlimited supply of video games, or even a place with no schools.

Instead, I found that for these students, utopia means a world where all are equal, where bullying is not a part of life, where power struggles are not necessary, where war is unheard of, where we all care about the earth and each other. I will always believe that adults have a lot to learn from children, if only we were patient listeners.

PSALM 147

1 Praise God. There is much joy in praising God, and in lifting our thanks to God. 2 God loves the city where peace reigns, where all are welcome. 3 God loves those who have been injured and healing is manifested in them. 4 God has a name for each star, even those that we cannot see. 5 God is absolute truth; there is no limit to God's knowledge. 6 God loves all, especially those who walk through their lives with humility. 7 Use your voice to praise God, sing songs of exaltation. 8 God created all the laws of nature, manifested as rain from the sky where it is needed. 9 There is food for all creatures, enough for all. 10 God's energy imbues us with strength of body, mind, and spirit. 11 The faithful give thanks for God's awesome powers. 12 Lift up songs of peace and love to God. 13 God's will is to love and protect all creatures. 14 Trust in God that God's peace and abundance are available to all who seek them. 15 While in prayer or meditation, God's wisdom is manifested. 16 Acts of nature are not random. Who does not believe in the laws of God's elegant design? 17 Water turns to ice. The cold ushers in a new season. 18 Then, in God's time, the frozen earth gives way to the green of Spring. 19 God's divine substance brings forth growth and abundance. 20 All are called to take part in God's divine plan. Praise God.

I don't know for certain who numbered the psalms, or put them in the order that they occupy, or even who decided on these 150 prayers and declared them part of a prayer book. Whoever it was decided to end the Psalter on a happy note and placed a series of praise psalms to remind us that God is to be revered and acclaimed.

Poets and composers thousands of years removed from me struggled with the same aspirations: hoping for peace, justice, respect for all of creations manifestations. I go to God with all of the faith I can muster, trusting in God's ability to empower me, to give me the will to work for a collective kindness towards all of God's creation.

PSALM 148

1 Praise God. Give thanks to God from the depths of the soul to the heights of the sky. 2 Praise God, all who serve God; praise God all creatures above and below. 3 All those who have been illumined by Spirit, whose mind is enlightened, praise God; praise God, all you who search for wisdom. 4 Praise for God rings from the firmament, from the source of rain and wind. 5 All of creation gives thanks to God, for without God there is nothingness, 6 no stars or planets, no sun or moon or earth. 7 From the depths of the oceans, where the great leviathan lives, 8 from the creatures who live with rain and snow and lightning, 9 from exalted minds and from those who trust in God, 10 from those who are beginners on the path to enlightenment, 11 from those whose lives are instructed by Spirit, 12 from young and old who follow God's plans. 13 Let all these give thanks and praise for God, who has set all of this in motion; whose substance manifests as the cosmos. 14 God and Spirit affirm that love and goodness surround creation and are available to all. Praise God.

As the Psalter comes to a close, the emphasis is on praising God. Whatever the poets could imagine as sources of laud and honor are called upon to express homage to God. Every part of creation, from our familiar sun to amorphous celestial minions, is commanded to acknowledge the Architect of ALL THAT IS. Whoever determined the order of the Psalms realized the importance of finishing this book with exultation.

The Psalms hold every joy and sorrow known to humans and they weave a grand tapestry of connections with our God – powerful stories told passionately and reverently.

Whether I think of Creation's origin as the Big Bang, or as pure thought from Divine Mind, or, better yet, both, I agree with the premise of number 148. Creation cannot be undone. I know that when my worldview comes to an end, my matter and energy will be dispersed to be used in ways that I cannot imagine today. It is an elegant system that holds us all.

"Praise God from whom all blessings flow."

PSALM 149

1 Give thanks and praise to God. Create a new song, to bring body, mind, and spirit into harmony. 2 All people who love God, celebrate God's presence; all people take delight in God's love. 3 Let all who love God sing God's praises and dance with joy. 4 God is within all of us. Let us be humble in God's honor. 5 Let all who love God show their faith in God's goodness with a song of rejoicing. 6 As we praise God with our words, let us not turn against another, 7 but let us greet all people with love and kindness, 8 and let us use our minds and hearts to benefit all. 9 Let us not stand in judgement of another, but let us seek to understand – this is what God calls us to do. Praise God.

As I approach the last psalm in each edition that I have studied, I am reluctant to see the book end. For me, these psalms have brought an awareness of God's constant presence, regardless of circumstances, or moods, or troubles, or sickness, or health. The psalms have softened me in places that badly needed attention, and given me strength when the fabric of my being was wearing thin.

There are so many opportunities in these psalms for self-reflection. For me they address the fundamental nature of my humanness, with all of its flaws and its gifts. I am given a chance to repent, or rejoice, or to simply wonder why I make certain choices. Then I can go into the silence and turn to God for insight.

This is the message for me: God loves me and I can lean into that love as far as I need to when I am in doubt, or am fearful. I am reminded that God has given me abilities, and opportunities to use them. And, I have been reminded I always have a choice between fear and faith, between doubt and hope.

PSALM 150

1 Praise God. God can be praised anywhere; where there is sun or moon, praise God. 2 Thank God for the gift of thought and imagination; praise God for the substance of creation. 3 Make music to honor God, let God's harmony resound throughout creation. 4 Let the energy of God's goodness thrive in body, mind and spirit. 5 Rejoice in the power of God's love and be grateful for it. 6 Let every living thing give thanks. Praise God.

So ends this voyage through the Psalms. This final message is about exultation and a heartfelt celebration of God and all God's gifts. I love that the last prayer asks that I use music as a way to express my love of God, that words alone are not the only connection between me and my creator.

All things considered, music is a fine way in which to give thanks and praise to God. The ability to put notes on a page and then translate them into sound is one manifestation of God's gift of creativity. For me, music is my quickest connection to Sprit. Really, though, any form of artistic expression can be seen as a prayer to creation.

God exists even in the tiny pauses between each note, between each breath that we take, in the middle of each heartbeat. Each living thing has its own rhythm and its own connection to God. And even when the time comes for that rhythm to cease, God carries all living things into the great unknown. We are each carried there with love. Praise God.

TOPICS

The Psalms are a rich source of assurance and affirmation in many areas of life. But the Psalms also address some negative aspects of human behavior. I have grouped the Psalms according to major categories that became clear as I wrote and re-read each psalm.

TOPIC	PSALM NUMBER
Abundance	20, 33, 49, 63, 65, 67, 73, 104, 123, 131, 132, 136, 137, 144, 147
Comfort Of God's Protection	3, 16, 17, 18, 23, 24, 27, 30, 31, 33, 35, 37, 40, 46, 54, 55, 89, 91, 104, 107, 110, 114, 116, 118, 121, 125, 126, 130, 131, 143, 144
Forgiveness	25, 32, 38, 51, 69, 79, 85, 86, 103, 109, 130
Glory Of God And Creation	8, 19, 29, 33, 50, 66, 84, 93, 95, 98, 100, 111, 138, 145, 147
God's Love	11, 33, 40, 48, 50, 68, 71, 75, 78, 89, 96, 103, 115, 116, 121, 127, 132, 136
God's Presence And Power	21, 23, 24, 31, 36, 40, 46, 55, 59, 62, 75, 78, 89, 90, 92, 97, 99, 104, 106, 108, 120, 129, 130, 133, 134, 137, 138, 139
Illness	6, 18, 38, 41, 43, 77, 88, 102, 116

Living A God-Centered Life	1, 9, 12, 15, 26, 34, 37, 39, 45, 47, 60, 61, 68, 71, 72, 76, 80, 82, 87, 89, 92, 97, 107, 112, 119, 128, 141, 144
Praising God	9, 30, 33, 50, 65, 67, 68, 75, 76, 81, 92, 95, 96, 100, 103, 105, 111, 113, 115, 117, 118, 128, 135, 145, 146, 147, 148, 149, 150
Prayer And Meditation	5, 17, 20, 23, 25, 26, 28, 30, 48, 55, 57, 60, 61, 66, 68, 70, 73, 81, 85, 86, 88, 91, 96, 97, 105, 110, 114, 122, 127, 141, 143
Spiritual Distress	4, 7, 13, 22, 31, 35, 38, 42, 43, 44, 54, 56, 69, 70, 73, 77, 86, 88, 102, 109, 124, 140, 142
Anger	55, 74
Arrogance	5, 10, 12, 14, 32, 36, 52, 53, 58, 73, 78, 83, 94, 106, 107, 140
Betrayal	35, 57, 109
Conflict	2, 35, 36, 55, 59, 64, 74, 79

SELECTED BIBLIOGRAPHY

Alter, Robert. *The Book of Psalms*. New York: W. W. Norton & Company, 2007.

Fillmore, Charles. *Metaphysical Bible Dictionary*. Unity Village: Unity Books, 2011.

Fillmore, Charles. *The Revealing Word*. Unity Village: Unity Books, 2006.

Fillmore, Myrtle. *How To Let God Help You*. Unity Village: Unity Books, 2006.

Stuhlmueller, Carroll. *The Spirituality of the Psalms*. Collegeville: The Liturgical Press, 2002.